The
Unknown Garden
of Another's Heart

The
Unknown Garden
of Another's Heart

The Surprising Friendship
between C.S. Lewis and Arthur Greeves

Joseph A. Kohm Jr.

WIPF & STOCK · Eugene, Oregon

Wipf & Stock
An Imprint of Wipf and Stock Publishers
199 W. 8th Ave., Suite 3
Eugene, OR 97401

www.wipfandstock.com

PAPERBACK ISBN: 978-1-6667-1039-7
HARDCOVER ISBN: 978-1-6667-1040-3
EBOOK ISBN: 978-1-6667-1041-0

VERSION NUMBER 010322

Unless otherwise noted, all Scripture quotations are from the Holy Bible, English Standard Version® (ESV®), copyright © 2001 by Crossway, a publishing ministry of Good News Publishers. All rights reserved.

For Lynne

"This is my beloved and this is my friend . . ."
—Song of Solomon 5:16

That we may mark with wonder and chaste dread
At hour of noon, when, with our limbs outspread
Lazily in the whispering grass, we lie
To gaze out fully upon the windy sky –
Far, far away, and kindly, friend with friend,
To talk the old, old talk that has no end,
Roaming – without a name – without a chart –
The unknown garden of another's heart.

—C. S. Lewis

Contents

Permissions

GRATEFUL ACKNOWLEDGEMENT IS MADE for permission to reprint the following material:

Permission to use Arthur Greeves's diaries has been kindly given by the owners of Arthur's diaries, the Marion E. Wade Center, located at Wheaton College, Wheaton, IL.

C. S. Lewis, *An Experiment in Criticism*, © Cambridge University Press 1961, Reproduced with permission of The Licensor through PLSclear.

They Stand Together: The Letters of C.S. Lewis to Arthur Greeves (1914–1963) by CS Lewis © copyright CS Lewis Pte Ltd 1979

Surprised by Joy: The Shape of My Early Life by CS Lewis © copyright CS Lewis Pte 1955

The Four Loves by CS Lewis © copyright CS Lewis Pte Ltd 1960

C.S. Lewis: The Companion & Guide, Walter Hooper © copyright CS Lewis Pte Ltd 1996

The Allegory of Love by CS Lewis © copyright CS Lewis Pte 1936

All My Road Before Me: The Diary of C.S. Lewis (1922 – 1927) by CS Lewis © copyright CS Lewis Pte Ltd 1991

Mere Christianity by CS Lewis © CS Lewis Pte Ltd 1942, 1943, 1944 1952

Acknowledgments

I AM ASHAMED TO say that I had never even heard of C. S. Lewis until my early thirties when I piled my wife and two young children into our car for a fourteen-hour trip to Cape Cod. I asked my wife what we were going to do to keep them occupied during the trip (this was before portable video players, cell phones, and iPads) and she said we were going to read the Chronicles of Narnia out loud. I told her I had never heard of them. Midway through *The Magician's Nephew* I turned to my wife and asked, "Who is this Lewis guy?" I was hooked, and so were my kids. I started a quest to read everything Lewis had written, and once I began reading his letters, I found Arthur Greeves everywhere. The more I learned about Arthur, the more intrigued I became with this beautiful and lifelong friendship. Those same two young children in the backseat of the car, Joe and Kathleen, along with my wife Lynne and I, have spent hours around our dinner table over the years discussing this friendship, and all things C. S. Lewis. Surprisingly, there is little written about the Arthur Greeves and C. S. Lewis friendship, so this is my humble attempt to shed light on an aspect of C. S. Lewis's life that deserves more attention.

In doing so, I am indebted to my boss at the C. S. Lewis Institute, Joel Woodruff, for his encouragement, prayers, and friendship. He is the best of men. I am also indebted to my colleague at the C. S. Lewis Institute Randy Newman, an exceptionally fine writer in his own right, for encouraging me as well. I want to thank Laura Schmidt at the Marion E. Wade Center for her assistance and kindness to me while researching the Arthur Greeves diaries. My sincere gratitude also extends to the following individuals: To my friend Becky Presnall, a gifted young poet and writer, who provided me with an idea when I was stuck. To my pastor, Fr. Andy Buchanan, of Galilee Episcopal Church in Virginia Beach, Virginia, who feeds me spiritually every Sunday. To my great friend Fr. Nigel Mumford of By His Wounds Ministry, who God used to heal me. To Jim Boeheim, Head Basketball Coach, Syracuse University, who taught me how to compete. To Walt Day from Cru's Athletes in Action, who introduced me to Jesus. To my uncle, Bill Kohm, for Tuesday updates. To my sisters, Buffy Boyce and Sarah Easton, who are strong, godly women and mothers. To my father and mother, Joe and Mary Kohm, for giving me life and being shining examples of what a mom and dad should be. To my children, Joe and Kathleen, who have made me proud each day of their lives. And finally, to my best friend and love of my life, my wife, Lynne Marie Kohm. To borrow a phrase from C. S. Lewis that he used about his relationship with Arthur Greeves, I am joined to you "like raindrops on a window."

CHAPTER 1

Introduction

IN APRIL OF 1914, a troubled fifteen-year-old boy, home for spring break from the school he hated, had just been given some good news. His father had informed him that he would only need to spend one more term at the school and then he would be allowed to leave and continue his education with the man who had tutored his older brother. Over the course of this young boy's short life, his older brother had been his only real friend. The two had grown up in a life of moderate affluence provided by their emotionally distant father, a solicitor. Their mother died of cancer in 1908, trampling the seeds of any faith in God the boy had. Growing up, both boys cocooned themselves in a life of books and drawing, creating their own imaginary world by bringing animals to life and calling their empire "Boxen." When the weather was fair, the brothers could explore the lush green hills of the Belfast, Ireland countryside.

Across the street lived a sickly young man of eighteen. Doctors told his parents when he was a small child that the boy had a heart condition. As a result, he lived a sedentary life, dropping out of formal schooling two years earlier. This afforded the young man the leisure of playing the piano, reading, and painting. His family ran a successful business converting material from flax plants into linen. The young man's father was stern, even "despotic,"[1] owing to the rigidity of the family's Plymouth Brethren faith. His mother was an enabler, trying to counteract the effects of his father's harshness. On this day, the young man was recovering from an illness and he inquired whether the boy across the street might be available to come visit him.

Up to this point, the boy and his older brother had attempted to avoid their neighbor "by every means in our power."[2] Yet on this day his older brother was away, and for some reason he decided to visit his convalescing neighbor. Upon entering the sick neighbor's room, the boy saw a copy of the book *Myths of the Norsemen*. "Do *you* like that?" the boy asked. Sitting up in his bed, the other replied, "Do *you* like that?" With Norse mythology providing the tinder, this meeting would produce a spark that would fan into a flame a friendship lasting almost fifty years. The boy would later write of that first encounter with his sick neighbor, "I had been so far from thinking such a friend possible that I had never even longed for one; no more than I longed to be King of England."[3]

By September 1963, the fifteen-year-old boy was now sixty-five and one of the world's most celebrated writers. In a little over two months, he would pass away at his home on the same very day as other world luminaries Aldous Huxley and United States President John F. Kennedy. Since that initial meeting with his sickly neighbor, he had fought in World War I, earned the academic distinction of a "Triple First" at Oxford, served both as a teaching fellow at Oxford's Magdalen College and as Professor of Medieval Renaissance English at Cambridge, appeared on the cover of *Time* magazine in the United States, published bestsellers in the genres of Christian apologetics, science fiction, and children's literature, and late in his life married a woman bed-ridden with cancer, who would eventually succumb to the disease four years later.

Now his health was deteriorating. He was largely confined to the first floor of his home on the outskirts of Oxford. Two years

---

1. Lewis, *They Stand Together*, 16.

2. Lewis, *Surprised by Joy*, 46.

3. Lewis, *Surprised by Joy*, 131.

earlier, he was scheduled for an operation to address the issue of a distended prostate gland.[4] Doctors were unable to proceed, as he also presented with a kidney infection and a weak heart. Two months earlier, he arrived at the same hospital for an examination relating to anemia and, moments after being admitted, he suffered a heart attack and slipped into a coma.[5] Miraculously, he survived, and he returned home three weeks later to be joined there under the constant supervision of a night nurse and his personal secretary. Penning the last of his 296 letters addressed to that sickly young man over the span of nearly fifty years, the famous writer concludes, "But oh Arthur, never to see you again! . . . Yours Jack"[6]

By now, the reader may have guessed the identity of one of the preceding individuals. C. S. Lewis is more popular now than ever before. His book *Mere Christianity* is arguably the most influential Christian work of the last one hundred years. Three of the seven books from the Chronicles of Narnia have been made into popular motion pictures. And on the fiftieth anniversary of his death, in 2013, Lewis was memorialized in Westminster Abby's Poets' Corner alongside such literary supernovas as Jane Austen and William Shakespeare.

Yet, who is the "Arthur" that C. S. Lewis laments he shall never see again? Arthur Joseph Greeves was born three and a half years earlier than Lewis on April 27, 1895, and lived across the road from the Lewis family. This book sets out to make the case that it was Arthur Greeves—not Owen Barfield, not J. R. R. Tolkien, and not even Lewis's brother Warnie—who was C. S. Lewis's best friend. The first of the 296 letters we have from Lewis to Arthur is from June 1914, and the last, referenced above, is dated September 11, 1963. Between these bookends, the remaining letters spanning nearly fifty years serve as an unrefracted light illuminating the life of C. S. Lewis, sometimes with shocking revelations. Those who want to see the unvarnished Lewis, warts and all, must begin here. In addition to the beautiful narrative of a fifty-year friendship,

---

4. Lewis, *Collected Letters*, 1:1278.

5. Lewis, *Collected Letters*, 1:1442.

6. Lewis, *Collected Letters*, 1:1456.

these letters lay out the trajectory of Lewis's faith journey from atheist to world-renowned apologist, ultimately and most importantly evincing a thoroughly transformed life. Conversely, readers are able to witness the almost opposite trajectory of Arthur Greeves's faith journey. Walter Hooper, who has served as the literary advisor to the Lewis estate since 1964, and who has been to Lewis what James Boswell was to Samuel Johnson, has written, "considering the intimacy and informality of their long friendship, I believe these letters may be as close as we shall ever get to Lewis himself."[7]

Some may wonder, "Where are all the letters from Arthur Greeves to C. S. Lewis?" There are two possible explanations of why only four letters from Arthur to C. S. Lewis remain. The first is that Lewis simply may not have retained them. Letter-writing took up a substantial portion of Lewis's day. "Oh the mails: every bore in two continents seems to think I like getting letters. One's real friends are precisely the people one never gets time to write to," Lewis complains to Dorothy Sayers.[8] Lewis, however, felt it was his duty to respond to each one. "I always answer fan-mail," he begins one letter, responding to an American admirer.[9] Lewis further elaborates on the situation regarding his mail in a letter to Arthur where he explains that in the "aftermath of those Broadcast Talks I gave early last summer I had an enormous pile of letters from strangers to answer. One gets funny letters after broadcasting – some from lunatics who sign themselves 'Jehovah' or begin 'Dear Mr. Lewis, I was married at the age of 20 to a man I didn't love' – but many from serious inquirers whom it was a duty to answer fully. So letter writing has loomed pretty large!"[10] With the enormous volume of correspondence Lewis received and sent out daily, he may have merely decided he didn't need the clutter.

A second and more likely explanation as to the letters from Arthur to C. S. Lewis concerns Lewis's brother, Warnie. Warnie

7. Lewis, *They Stand Together*, 12.
8. Lewis, *Collected Letters*, 1:1014.
9. Lewis, *Collected Letters*, 1:641.
10. Lewis, *Collected Letters*, 1:504.

was devastated by his brother's death. Shortly thereafter, he decided to move out of the Kilns, the home he had shared with his bother since 1930, and into a smaller residence. Prone to debilitating bouts of alcoholism, Warnie, Walter Hooper records, once "kept a bonfire of papers burning for three days."[11] Shortly after Lewis's death, Hooper went out to the Kilns to check on Warnie and was able to rescue the four letters from Arthur before they, "Warren assured me, would have gone into the fire."[12] Hooper surmises that it is entirely possible that if they existed, all other letters from Arthur to C. S. Lewis were incinerated in the three-day burn.

Fortunately, we are able to reconstruct much of the content and subject matter between the two from Lewis's letters alone. As a letter writer, even at an early age, Lewis habitually restated pertinent information from the last letter he received from the sender to build upon the content within the letter he was drafting. This literary device would serve him well later in his books that centered around the use of letters, such as *The Screwtape Letters* and *Letters to Malcolm: Chiefly on Prayer*.

Located within the story of friendship between Lewis and Greeves that these 296 letters tell are all the major life events Lewis scholars and fans are familiar with. He writes to Arthur about his relationship with Janie Moore (mother of his friend Paddy Moore), on Warnie's chronic alcoholism, on his conversion to Christianity, on his marriage to Joy Davidman, and on his impending death, evincing why Walter Hooper makes the claim regarding these letters that those who really wish to know him will find the real Lewis within. Though it ebbed and flowed over the course of their respective lives, the relationship was indispensable to each. To the outsider, it would be reasonable to ask why Lewis, one of the most accomplished men of the twentieth century, would befriend, let alone be best friends with, someone like Arthur Greeves, who lived a very ordinary life. Who was Arthur Greeves, and why did he hold such a place in C. S. Lewis's heart that Lewis was once compelled to write, "when I come to die I am more likely to remember certain

11. Lewis, *They Stand Together*, 42.
12. Lewis, *They Stand Together*, 42.

things that you and I have explored or suffered or enjoyed together than anything else."[13]

Much of what is known about Arthur Greeves is attributable to both Warnie and C. S. Lewis. While Warnie's vocation was in the military, he was an accomplished author in his own right, publishing books on French history. He also devoted a significant effort to chronicling "The Memoirs of the Lewis Family: 1850–1930," which ultimately produced eleven volumes with over three hundred pages each, containing letters, photographs, and other family documents. C. S. Lewis made two written contributions to the effort that are pertinent here. The first installment, recorded in 1933, paints an unflattering portrait of the Greeves family. He describes Greeves's father as "a harsh husband and a despotic father."[14] Greeves's mother had an outer veneer that was "simple, warm hearted," but underneath "a genuine streak of ill nature in her."[15] After her husband's death, Lewis writes that "Her conversation came to consist more and more of a perpetual attempt, and a perpetual failure, to tell stories and riddles."[16] Lewis notes that the family's faith was rooted in the Plymouth Brethren and that each of the family's five children ultimately abandoned that faith, with the result being that "their upbringing gave them no HUMANE tradition to turn to when once their theology was gone."[17]

Arthur was the youngest of five children. Early in his life he was diagnosed with a bad heart. Unable to work, he lived as what would today be called a trust fund baby, as his family's flax-spinning business was prosperous. He achieved some success as a painter, studying at the Slade School of Fine Art in London as well as having his paintings exhibited with the Royal Hiberian Academy in Dublin.[18]

13. Lewis, *They Stand Together*, 370.

14. Lewis, *They Stand Together*, 16.

15. Lewis, *They Stand Together*, 17.

16. Lewis, *They Stand Together*, 17.

17. Lewis, *They Stand Together*, 18.

18. Duriez, *C. S. Lewis Encyclopedia*, 84.

Several years later, Lewis made another addition to "The Memoirs of the Lewis Family," this time focusing solely on Arthur. According to Lewis, Arthur tended "towards self-pity." He was also "the frankest of men," and "never showed any inclination to revenge himself." To his detriment, Arthur could easily be swayed to "adopt any canon of taste." Also, according to Lewis, Arthur failed to acquire the "visor to the human face,"[19] a characteristic embedded in men as a consequence of life's experience, resulting in an outward façade of toughness.

We can also learn about Arthur in his own words from the diaries he kept during 1917 and 1918 and then for a short period in 1922. These diaries are kept at the Marion E. Wade Center at Wheaton College in Wheaton, Illinois. They reveal an anxious and lonely young man. Not being able to work, he describes his days as consisting of meeting various people for lunch, reading in the garden, having tea, and attending church. Evidence of C. S. Lewis's description of Arthur's father as "harsh" and "despotic" in "The Memoirs of the Lewis Family" are reflected in Arthur's entries regarding his father. A major point of contention seems to have been be Arthur's allowance. An entry from April 23, 1917, notes, "Talk with father, seems hopeless. I trust in God. All will turn out right."[20] During the summer of 1922, Arthur pressed his father concerning a regular allowance but was rebuffed, with Arthur describing his father's response as "most unattractive to put it mildly – said certainly not."[21] This entry concludes with Arthur writing that his father "shunned me as no Christian man – much less father would do."[22]

Arthur's diary entries also reveal him attempting to make his faith his own. He was confirmed on June 10, 1917, in "stifling

---

19. Lewis, *They Stand Together*, 24.

20. Arthur Greeves diary entry, April 23, 1917, Arthur Greeves Diaries Collection, folder 1 (Marion E. Wade Center, Wheaton College, Wheaton, IL).

21. Arthur Greeves diary entry, July 23, 1922, Arthur Greeves Diaries Collection, folder 8 (Marion E. Wade Center, Wheaton College, Wheaton, IL).

22. Arthur Greeves diary entry, July 23, 1922, Arthur Greeves Diaries Collection, folder 8 (Marion E. Wade Center, Wheaton College, Wheaton, IL).

heat."[23] He regularly records whether he had attended church, and various entries contain heartfelt mini-prayers such as, "Pray God I may keep pure minded."[24] But one subject appears more than any other, and that is his friend Jack Lewis. There is a repetitive fixation on whether he received daily correspondence from Lewis. Arthur's diaries also coincide with Lewis's military service during World War I, where Lewis was seriously injured, and naturally Arthur displays a heightened level of concern for his friend.

Reading Arthur's diaries also show him to be intelligent and sensitive. For Lewis, the most attractive personal characteristic of Arthur's was rooted in what Lewis calls the "homely." Arthur's enjoyment of the ordinary was his sustenance. "A bright hearth seen through an open door as we passed, a train of ducks following a brawny farmer's wife, a drill of cabbages in a suburban garden – these were the things that never failed to move him, even to an ecstasy."[25] In a 1931 letter to Arthur where Lewis informs him that he has "just passed on from believing in God to definitely believing in Christ – in Christianity," Lewis tells Arthur that "homeliness" was the chief lesson he learned from him and how this "homeliness" was an introduction to the Christian virtue of charity or love.[26]

Lewis realized the power of friendship early in his life as a talisman against the brutality of the headmaster of Wynyard School, where he was sent at age ten to further his education, a mere four weeks after his mother died. In his autobiography, *Surprised by Joy*, Lewis tags the Wynyard School with the moniker "Belsen" after the Nazi concentration camp.[27] The headmaster, Robert Capron, administered relentless floggings, with Lewis reporting he witnessed

---

23. Arthur Greeves diary entry, June 10, 1917, Arthur Greeves Diaries Collection, folder 2 (Marion E. Wade Center, Wheaton College, Wheaton, IL).

24. Arthur Greeves diary entry, July 8, 1917, Arthur Greeves Diaries Collection, folder 2 (Marion E. Wade Center, Wheaton College, Wheaton, IL).

25. Lewis, *They Stand Together*, 25.

26. Lewis, *They Stand Together*, 425.

27. Lewis, *Surprised by Joy*, 24.

Capron take running starts to deliver blows.[28] One boy's parents brought an action against Capron for abuse, and he ultimately was committed to an asylum, where he died in 1911. Upon Lewis's arrival, there were approximately nine students who were boarding at the school, and another nine who were day students. As Capron's mental condition worsened, attendance dwindled until there were just five remaining boarders.[29] It was within this remnant that Lewis found the strength to withstand his remaining days at Wynyard. "We stood foursquare against the common enemy. I suspect this pattern . . . has unduly biased my whole outlook. To this day the vision of the world which comes most naturally to me is one in which 'we two' or 'we few' (and in a sense 'we happy few') stand together against something stronger and larger."[30]

The weight and importance Lewis placed on the idea of friendship led to one of the more significant relationships over the course of his life. England was engaged in World War I, and on June 8, 1917, Lewis joined the army. While billeted in Keble College, Oxford, he roomed with another Irishman named Edward Francis Courtney "Paddy" Moore. A few months later, Lewis spent his leave time at Paddy's home. It was there that he first met Paddy's mother, Janie King Moore. During this visit, Lewis and Paddy Moore promised each other that if one of them were killed in the war, the survivor would look after the other's parent.[31] Sadly, Paddy Moore died in March 1918 when the Germans recaptured the French city of Peronne.[32]

Lewis fulfilled his end of the bargain with Paddy. He was wounded in battle (by friendly fire) on April 15, 1918, and after his convalescence he lived with Mrs. Moore in Oxford from 1919 until her death on January 12, 1951. The general consensus among Lewis scholars is that he was both sexually and romantically involved with Mrs. Moore for an extended period of time.

28. Lewis, *Surprised by Joy*, 27.

29. Lewis, *Surprised by Joy*, 31.

30. I Lewis, *Surprised by Joy*, 32.

31. Zaleski and Zaleski, *Fellowship*, 79.

32. Zaleski and Zaleski, *Fellowship*, 80.

After his conversion to Christianity, the nature of their relationship changed, with Lewis often referring to her in correspondence as his "Mother."[33] Mrs. Moore had been previously married, then separated, but never divorced. Later in her life she suffered from dementia.[34] Lewis dutifully cared for her at home for a period of time before placing her in a nursing home in the spring of 1950. Janie Moore died a few months later on January 12, 1951.

Those seeking to fully understand C. S. Lewis must understand the significance and weight he placed on the concept of friendship. The core of Lewis's beliefs regarding friendship was that it "must be about something."[35] For Lewis, this meant, "Do you see the same truth?"[36] When C. S. Lewis walked into Arthur Greeves's bedroom in the spring of 1914 and saw Arthur with *Myths of the Norsemen*, Lewis knew he and Arthur saw the same truth. Seeing this same truth was the foundation that their friendship was built upon. Seeing this same truth is what allowed, to the outside observer, an internationally known and accomplished intellectual like C. S. Lewis to be best friends with a relatively unknown and seemingly unaccomplished person like Arthur Greeves.

In addition to seeing the same truth, there was another factor in play that helps explain the friendship of C. S. Lewis and Arthur Greeves. It is a factor in all friendships and Lewis points it out in his book *The Four Loves*: "But for a Christian, there are, strictly speaking, no chances. A secret Master of Ceremonies has been at work. Christ, who said to the disciples 'Ye have not chosen me, but I have chosen you,' can truly say to every group of Christian friends 'You have not chosen one another but I have chosen you for one another.'"[37] When C. S. Lewis walked into Arthur's bedroom that spring morning in 1914, it was no mere accident, no mere chance. From the beginning of time, God had ordained their friendship, just as God has ordained all our friendships. The

33. Hooper, *C. S. Lewis*, 714.

34. Jacobs, *Narnian*, 250.

35. Lewis, *Four Loves*, 66.

36. Lewis, *Four Loves*, 66.

37. Lewis, *Four Loves*, 89.

friendship between C. S. Lewis and Arthur is one of the many examples of "all things" working together for good (Romans 8:28), the good here being that seventy years later readers are still learning from C. S. Lewis.

CHAPTER 2

"Galahad"

THE YOUNG C. S. Lewis brought preconceived notions about what friendship looks like into his newfound friendship with Arthur Greeves. These ideas about friendship had been formed by his relationship with his older brother, Warnie, and by his experiences at the various schools he had attended before meeting Arthur. In 1905, Lewis's father, Albert, built the family a new home on the outskirts of Belfast that was affectionately called "Little Lea." At Little Lea, young "Jack," as he liked to be called, and Warnie spent much of their time in their attic playroom devising and constructing imaginary worlds. It was not long though before Warnie was sent away to the Wynard School in Hertfordshire, England, leaving Lewis without the only friend he had known. It was not that other children in the neighborhood hadn't tried to befriend the Lewis brothers. Lewis writes in his autobiography *Surprised by Joy* that "One boy who lived near us attempted every now and then to get to know us."[1] Presumably, this boy was Arthur Greeves, yet Jack and Warnie "avoided him by every means in our power."[2] Rebuffing overtures from other children "was the result of our own obstinate choice." Warnie's time at home was too short between academic terms and interlopers would have just infringed on their

1. Lewis, *Surprised by Joy*, 46.
2. Lewis, *Surprised by Joy*, 46.

plans. "We resented the appearance of any third party as an infuriating interruption."[3]

While his only friend, Warnie, was away at school, Lewis was tutored at home by his mother, Flora, and governess, Annie Harper.[4] In his free time, he roamed the long corridors and empty sunlit rooms of Little Lea. His sole companions were the "endless books" his father purchased, which filled nearly every available space in the house. Topically, Albert and Flora Lewis read broadly, and Lewis was permitted access to all of it, which allowed him to stretch the imaginative borders of his active mind. Sadly, Lewis's pleasant childhood came to an abrupt stop in 1908 when his mother was diagnosed with cancer. Flora Lewis died at home just a few months later, and by September little Jack found himself on a boat with Warnie heading across the Irish Sea. Their destination was the Wynyard School, where Warnie had been a student the previous three years.

Lewis's time at Wynyard School was formative in shaping his views on friendship, primarily due to the horrific conditions he encountered there. The school was run by Robert Capron, his wife, and their three daughters. Capron founded Wynyard in 1882 and by the time Lewis arrived the number of students included seven or eight boarders with about the same number of day students, down from as many as thirty in the school's heyday. The students nicknamed him "Oldie" behind his back, and Lewis was immediately baptized into his sadistic teaching methods. In *Surprised by Joy*, Lewis remembers Capron having a boy bent over on one side of the room with Capron getting a running start from the other side of the room to deliver a blow with a cane.[5]

Episodes like this produced "grey faces of all the other boys, and their deathlike stillness," forging in a crucible of terror Lewis's early view of friendship. Withstanding Capron's brutal behavior forced the students to congeal together, "foursquare against the common enemy. I suspect this pattern, occurring twice" (the first

---

3. Lewis, *Surprised by Joy*, 46.
4. McGrath, *C. S. Lewis*, 17.
5. Lewis, *Surprised by Joy*, 27.

time for Lewis was drawing closer with Warnie after their mother died), "and so early in my life, has unduly biased my whole outlook. To this day the vision of the world which comes most naturally to me is one in which 'we two' or 'we few' . . . stand together against something stronger and larger."[6]

Wynyard School was closed in the summer of 1910 after Robert Capron was found to be insane. Albert Lewis then arranged to have Jack attend a school closer to home in Belfast in the fall of 1910, but after only one term Lewis contracted a respiratory virus and that forced Albert to withdraw the young Lewis. To continue his education, his father sent him back across the Irish Sea to England to a prep school, Cherbourg House, located in Great Malvern. As Lewis entered his teenage years, he became susceptible to the same cultural influences that pull at today's teenagers—fashion, music, and humor.

One of Cherbourg's masters was a young man Lewis identifies in *Surprised by Joy* as "Pogo."[7] Lewis recalls, "Here was sophistication, glossy all over, and (dared one believe it?) ready to impart sophistication to us."[8] Pogo taught his young charges "all the latest songs" and "all the latest jokes." In addition, Lewis finds that he had become "dressy." "I cannot even now remember without embarrassment the concern that I felt about pressing my trousers and (filthy habit) plastering my hair with oil."[9] Lewis's concern for his appearance was a part of what all teenagers seek, acceptance from their peers, a process usually coupled with the development of their own identity.

The next step in Lewis's educational journey was Malvern College. While not a "college" in the sense that twenty-first-century Westerners think of college, in the nineteenth-century English educational system Malvern was the equivalent of what we would consider high school. Warnie had preceded Jack at Malvern, but by the time Lewis arrived Warnie was gone.

6. Lewis, *Surprised by Joy*, 32.

7. Lewis, *Surprised by Joy*, 67.

8. Lewis, *Surprised by Joy*, 67.

9. Lewis, *Surprised by Joy*, 66.

Upon his arrival at Malvern, Lewis entered a hierarchal social system and at the very apex of the Malvern structure were the "Bloods." The most important quality possessed by a Blood was "athletic prowess," followed by "good looks" and "fashion."[10] Bloods were afforded special privileges not available to others. Today, we might identify Bloods in the adolescent hierarchy with spoiled high school quarterbacks.

Another group in the Malvern system was the "Tarts." It is here that Lewis pulls back the curtain on an element of the English educational system that rightly offends contemporary sensibilities. The prevalence of pederasty, or same-sex intimacy between an older male and younger boy, was a part of the English educational process during that period. Lewis describes a Tart as "a pretty and effeminate-looking boy who acts as a catamite to one or more of his seniors, usually Bloods."[11]

Lewis did not fit in to the Malvern system because he "hated games,"[12] was naturally clumsy, and had a perpetual look on his face that others interpreted as defiant and arrogant.[13] In addition, he quickly got off on the wrong foot when an upperclassman purposely told Lewis he was to report to one group of students for the school's compulsory games when in fact Lewis had been assigned to a different group. This caused Lewis to commit the offense of "Skipping Clubs," for which he was subjected to the punishment of a flogging.[14] Compounding Lewis's hatred of Malvern was the process where older students, usually Bloods, made junior students serve them by completing menial jobs such as polishing their shoes or cleaning their rooms. This system was known as "fagging" and the extra duties caused Lewis to be perpetually exhausted, cutting into valuable time that he could have used for his studies. Lewis describes the ultimate effect Malvern had on him—it caused him to become a prig.

10. Lewis, *Surprised by Joy*, 84.
11. Lewis, *Surprised by Joy*, 86.
12. Lewis, *Surprised by Joy*, 90.
13. Lewis, *Surprised by Joy*, 94.
14. Lewis, *Surprised by Joy*, 90.

When C. S. Lewis walked into Arthur Greeves's room that April day in 1914, he carried with him the belief that the foundation of friendship was constructed on standing against something, whether it be third-party interlopers, grief at losing his beloved mother, the verbal and physical abuse aimed at him and his fellow students by a mentally unbalanced school master, or the experience of consistently being treated as the low person on the totem pole among his school peers. Lewis was near to completing his time at Malvern when he first met with Arthur Greeves. He had begged his father to allow him to leave Malvern after just one year, and his father acquiesced. Other than his brother, Warnie, Lewis had no other close friends.

On that fateful day in April, word had somehow reached Lewis at Little Lea that his neighbor Arthur Greeves was sick and would very much appreciate a visit from him. A few years earlier, Lewis had been captivated by the idea of "Northerness" after viewing an illustration from the book *Siegfried and the Twilight of the Gods* at school. For Lewis, "Northerness" encompassed the "vision of huge, clear spaces hanging above the Atlantic in the endless twilight of Northern summer, remoteness, severity."[15] Thus, when Lewis walked into Arthur's bedroom and found him sitting up in bed with a copy of the book *Myths of the Norsemen* on the table beside him, there was a flurry of activity. They were soon "pointing, quoting, talking – soon almost shouting – discovering in a torrent of questions that we liked not only the same thing, but the same parts of it and in the same way."[16] This meeting provided Lewis with a "stab of Joy and that, for both, the arrow was shot from the North."[17] For the first time, Lewis came to the welcome realization that there were other boys who were very like himself.

This excitement in discovering that there was someone else who liked the same things he liked can be found in his very first letter to Arthur. Written during what must have been his last few weeks at Malvern, Lewis, exhibiting the priggishness he admitted

15. Lewis, *Surprised by Joy*, 73.
16. Lewis, *Surprised by Joy*, 130.
17. Lewis, *Surprised by Joy*, 130.

Malvern produced in him, complains to Arthur that what bothers him most about the school "is the absolute lack of appreciation of anything like music or books which prevails among the people whom I am forced to call my companions."[18] While reflecting that same priggishness, Lewis tells Arthur the benefit of attending Malvern is that it has taught him that had he not ever "seen the horrible spectacle which these coarse, brainless English schoolboys present, there might be a danger of my sometimes becoming like that myself."[19]

Lewis's exit from Malvern meant that his father needed to find a new locus for his son's education. Recently, Albert Lewis had sent Warnie to be tutored by Albert's old headmaster at Lurgan College, William Kirkpatrick.[20] Kirkpatrick was now doing some private tutoring and living in the village of Great Bookham, located in Surrey, England. Albert was pleased with the results from Warnie's time with Kirkpatrick, helping Warnie gain acceptance to England's prestigious military academy at Sandhurst, and he asked Kirkpatrick to take in and tutor young Jack.

Lewis arrived in Great Bookham in September of 1914. Affectionately known as "the Great Knock" among the Lewis men,[21] Kirkpatrick attended a Presbyterian seminary earlier in his life but was now and atheist.[22] The laser-sharp logician's atheism served as a refining fire, burning away the educational impurities Lewis previously acquired and providing Lewis with an atmosphere where he could really be happy and flourish. After feeding Lewis a steady diet of languages and the classics, Kirkpatrick soon realized what he had in Lewis. Writing to Albert, Kirkpatrick gushed, "He has read more classics than any boy I ever had – or indeed I might add than any I ever heard of, unless it be an Addison or Landor, or

---

18. Lewis, *They Stand Together*, 47.
19. Lewis, *They Stand Together*, 47.
20. McGrath, *C. S. Lewis*, 30.
21. Lewis, *Surprised by Joy*, 133.
22. Hooper, *C. S. Lewis*, 9.

Macaulay. These are people we read of, but I have never met any . . . He is the most brilliant translator of Greek plays I have ever met."[23]

Lewis's happiness with his situation at Great Bookham is reflected in his second letter to Arthur, where he writes, "I have come to the conclusion that I am going to have the time of my life."[24] His days were spent reading the *Iliad*, learning Latin, and following a reading course prescribed by Kirkpatrick. In his free time, he composed his own operatic story, *Loki Bound*, centered around the Norse god Loki. In his third letter to Arthur, Lewis provides him with an outline of the plot and invites Arthur to compose a musical score to go along with the story in the hopes they can turn *Loki Bound* into an opera.

As the pace of their correspondence quickened, what developed over the next three years was the unveiling of each to the other. Lewis set the conditions for their letter-writing early in the relationship, telling Arthur that their letters to each other should consist of three things: "doings," "readings," and "thinkings."[25] The "doings" in Lewis's early letters to Arthur consist of his daily schedule. He was awakened in the morning by Kirkpatrick using the bathroom. Then, after breakfast and a walk, he began his studies until lunch. His afternoons were free until 5 p.m., when he began again working with Kirkpatrick until 9 p.m. with dinner interspersed at 7:30 p.m. Instead of going straight to bed, Lewis spent time sitting at his desk trying to "produce," either by sketching, writing poetry or short stories, or writing in his diary.[26] Another of Lewis's "doings" included spending time in what he describes as a "Soaking-machine," which was a secluded spot at the foot of a large oak tree, where he was shielded from the elements and where, with notebook and pencil in hand, he was free to write as he pleased.

Lewis's "readings" make up a staggering portion of the content of his early letters to Arthur. As discussed earlier, Lewis's

23. Jacobs, *Narnian*, 58–59.
24. Lewis, *Collected Letters*, 1:70.
25. Lewis, *Collected Letters*, 1:92.
26. Lewis, *Collected Letters*, 1:146.

habits as a reader were developed early in his life and fostered by the seemingly endless supply of books found in his childhood home Little Lea. By age ten, Lewis was reading Milton's *Paradise Lost*,[27] and for the remainder of his life reading was as life-giving for Lewis as oxygen. He was once described by William Empson as "the best-read man of his generation, one who read everything and remembered everything he read."[28] Supporting evidence for this claim can be found in the fact that the collected three-volume set of his letters contain over twelve thousand quotations or references to books Lewis had read throughout his life.[29]

In addition to continually updating Arthur on what he was reading, Lewis had a fixation on books themselves, their binding, how they looked, the type of paper used. For Lewis, the look and feel of a book was almost as important as the content. This was something that he learned from Arthur. In *Surprised by Joy* Lewis credits Arthur with teaching him to love the bodies of books, "But Arthur did not merely respect (books), he was enamored; and soon, I too. The setup of the page, the feel and smell of the paper, the differing sounds that different papers make as soon as you turn the leaves, become sensuous delights."[30] So foundational were books and music to Lewis that, in a 1916 letter to Arthur, Lewis responds incredulously to Arthur's "hurt" feelings about Lewis restricting the content of his letters to mainly these two topics by writing, "But seriously, what can you have been thinking about when you said 'only' books, music, etc., just as these weren't real things!"[31]

In a letter to Arthur many years later, Lewis describes his praxis for reading. With pen in hand, he had made a map on one of the end leaves of the book and "put a running headline at the top of each page: finally I index at the end all the passages I have for

---

27. Lewis, *Reading Life*, xi.

28. Como, ed., *C. S. Lewis*, xxiii.

29. Lewis, *Reading Life*, xii.

30. Lewis, *Surprised by Joy*, 164.

31. Lewis, *Collected Letters*, 1:205.

any reason underlined."[32] His efforts at annotation were probably unnecessary as Lewis had a photographic memory. His students remember him being able to recall lengthy passages of books and poetry. His sheer intensity as a reader was pointed out by Dame Helen Gardner, who was the second choice for Cambridge University's Professor in Medieval and Renaissance English in 1954, a position that C. S. Lewis accepted. In her obituary of Lewis, Gardner recalled that seeing Lewis reading in the Bodleian Library at Oxford "was to have an object lesson in what concentration meant. He seemed to create a wall of stillness around him."[33]

The final requirement of Lewis's letter-writing conditions with Arthur included "thinkings." The content of these "thinkings" found in the early letters between C. S. Lewis and Arthur Greeves probably mirror the content found in texts messages of many of today's male millennials. But for those not familiar with C. S. Lewis's background and faith journey, who only know him as the author of *Mere Christianity* or the creator of the Chronicles of Narnia, these revelations may come as a shock. Religion, sex, and alcohol are each present. These early letters are particularly instructive as they reveal Lewis's views on religion. As discussed previously, Lewis had some form of faith as a young child, however, after the death of his mother, he drifted away from the Christian faith and by the time he began corresponding with Arthur, he was a confirmed atheist, a fact that he hid from his father. Just a few months into his tutelage with Kirkpatrick, Lewis's father recalled him home to Belfast for a week of religious instruction so that Lewis could be confirmed in the family's home church, St. Mark's. Lewis would later refer to his confirmation as "one of the worst acts of my life. I allowed myself to be prepared for confirmation, and confirmed, and to make my first Communion in total disbelief."[34]

It appears that Arthur, who at that time in his life identified as a Christian, was the first to interject the subject of religion into their letters. In a letter dated October 12, 1916, Lewis writes, "You

32. Lewis, *They Stand Together*, 438.
33. Hooper, *C. S. Lewis*, 55.
34. Lewis, *Surprised by Joy*, 161.

ask me my religious views."[35] Years later, Lewis drafted a written portrait of Arthur for the project undertaken by Warnie to compose the Lewis family history, resulting in "The Memoirs of the Lewis Family: 1850–1930," mentioned earlier. In this portrait of Arthur, he remembers that early in their friendship, "though (God forgive me), I bombarded him with all the thin artillery of a seventeen year old rationalist."[36] The projectiles launched by Lewis in his bombardment of Arthur's faith consisted of a lengthy rebuke of religion in general and a quick dismissal of Christianity. Lewis tells Arthur that "There is absolutely no proof" for any religion, that they are based on superstition.[37] As for Jesus, Lewis labels him a "Hebrew philosopher" who became the source of a cult, just "one mythology among many."[38] In his subsequent letter to Arthur, Lewis expands his thoughts on Jesus, admitting he existed but dismissing "all the other tomfoolery about virgin birth, magic healings, apparitions, and so forth."[39] Lewis goes so far as to admit his sadness that he had been unable to deconvert Arthur, hoping that Arthur was "gradually escaping from beliefs which, in my case, always considerably lessened my happiness."[40]

In addition to religion, another "thinking" that not surprisingly preoccupied young men like C. S. Lewis and Arthur Greeves was sex, a topic that found its way early on into their friendship. In just Lewis's eleventh letter to Arthur, he excitedly describes an upcoming amorous rendezvous with a Belgian girl, who, along with her mother, had fled the chaos of World War I in her home country for England. Over a quarter of a million Belgians made their way to the United Kingdom during World War I, with between two and three thousand refugees being located near Lewis in Great Bookham.[41] Lewis met this young lady through Mrs.

---

35. Lewis, *Collected Letters*, 1:230.
36. Lewis, *They Stand Together*, 25.
37. Lewis, *Collected Letters*, 1:230.
38. Lewis, *Collected Letters*, 1:231.
39. Lewis, *Collected Letters*, 1:234.
40. Lewis, *Collected Letters*, 1:235.
41. Poe, *Becoming C. S. Lewis*, 178.

Kirkpatrick, who had been visiting the refugees, and Lewis had told Arthur about his feeling for the girl a few weeks before while home for Christmas. In a letter dated February 2, 1915, it appears that their relationship status had accelerated. Lewis writes, "we have progressed very rapidly. In fact the great event is fixed – fixed! – do you realize that? I don't think I've ever been so bucked about anything in my life, she's an awfully decent sort."[42] We are not told specifically what the "great event" was that Lewis refers to. The insinuation is that Lewis and this young woman were, in modern terminology, going to "hook up." Alas, in Lewis's next letter, he tells Arthur that the "great event" had never materialized. For a reason Lewis fails to explain, he had not shown up for his date with this girl, which appears to have severed the budding relationship.[43]

Conversely, Arthur's sexual mores at that time must have been more puritan, as evidenced by a nickname Lewis gives him a few weeks later. Over the course of the next year, most of the salutations in Lewis's letters label Arthur as "Galahad," apparently after Sir Galahad, a knight of King Arthur's Round Table, who was able to locate the Holy Grail because of his purity. It appears that Arthur reciprocated with his own nickname for Lewis—"Chubs."[44]

As their friendship progressed during this period, the topic of sex became more frequent. While at Great Bookham, Lewis writes Arthur that, while Arthur won't have to listen to another of Lewis's love affairs, he has "met the prettiest girl I have ever seen in my life," comparing her appearance and speech to a piece of music.[45] Arthur apparently responded by asking whether Lewis had ever been in love. Lewis responds that he had not, writing, "I am not quite such as fool as all that."[46] But, while personally not having been in love, Lewis tells Arthur he has experienced something even better in that he has experienced love as a reader through the eyes of writers like Jane Austen, Charlotte Bronte, and Edmund

42. Lewis, *Collected Letters*, 1:105.

43. Lewis, *Collected Letters*, 1:108.

44. Lewis, *Collected Letters*, 1:190.

45. Lewis, *Collected Letters*, 1:129.

46. Lewis, *Collected Letters*, 1:146.

Spenser. This early idea that reading allows one to see and experience the world through the eyes of others would be foundational to Lewis his whole life. In 1961, Lewis concludes his book *An Experiment in Criticism* with, "But in reading great literature I become a thousand men and yet remain myself. Like the night sky in the Greek poem, I see with a myriad eyes, but it is still I who see. Here, as in worship, in love, in moral action, and in knowing, I transcend myself: and am never more myself than when I do."[47] For his part, Arthur defined romantic love as the combination of friendship and sensual feelings, but Lewis disagrees, believing at that time that love can encompass only one, but not both.[48] Arthur may have also revealed to Lewis that he had a crush on someone, prompting Lewis to respond, "I am sorry to hear of your infatuation (very much inFATuation) for a certain lady, but you need not despair, nor do I propose to call you out; we will divide mother & daughter between us, and you can have first choice!"[49]

In addition to its increased frequency, the treatment of the topic of sex began to take a darker turn. Over the first six months of 1917, Lewis's letters to Arthur contain references to his flirtation with sadism. For those who know C. S. Lewis primarily as the author of *Mere Christianity* or the Chronicles of Narnia, the contents of these letters can be shocking. It is important to remember, however, that these letters were written long before Lewis became a devoted follower of Christ, and there is not one of us who would not be ashamed or embarrassed at forty or fifty by something we wrote or said at age nineteen.

Just a few weeks before this series of letters, in early December of 1916, Lewis had gone to Oxford to sit for a scholarship examination. While back home for Christmas vacation, he heard from University College within Oxford University that he had been awarded a scholarship. This did not mean he was admitted to Oxford. Lewis took a trip back to Oxford in January of 1917, where he met with the master of University College, Reginald Macan, at

---

47. Lewis, *Experiment in Criticism*, 141.
48. Lewis, *Collected Letters*, 1:146.
49. Lewis, *Collected Letters*, 1:259.

his home.[50] Macan told Lewis that if he passed Responsions, commonly known as "Little Go," Lewis could begin at Oxford that summer in the Trinity term. Lewis then headed back to Great Bookham to begin preparing for the exam.

In his first letter to Arthur upon returning to Great Bookham, Lewis recounts his trip to Oxford and his meeting with Reginald Macan. Beginning with, "My dear Galahad, (If you are still to be Galahad after all),"[51] Lewis describes how he went to Macan's home, where Macan invited him to stay for lunch. Also present were Macan's wife and niece, who Lewis describes as being "very decent, indeed the latter wouldn't be a bad subject for the lash."[52] Toward the conclusion of the letter, Lewis mentions he has been writing it across his knee, which triggers the following commentary: "'Across my knee' of course makes one think of positions for Whipping: or rather not for whipping (you couldn't get any swing) but for that torture with brushes. This position, with its childish, nursery associations wd. have something beautifully intimate and also very humiliating for the victim."[53]

Subsequent letters include Lewis's interest in punishing a member of Arthur's family, "to the general enjoyment of the operator, and to the great good of her soul,"[54] concluding the letter with the signature "Philomastix," which means "lover of the rod."[55] There is a general coarsening and baseness as the train of this subject devolves. Apparently, Arthur had told Lewis he would be more interested in "suffering" rather than "inflicting."[56] In another letter, Lewis shares similar revelation, identifying with Jean-Jacques Rousseau's experiences in Rousseau's autobiographical *The Confessions*.[57]

50. Poe, *Becoming C. S. Lewis*, 236.

51. Lewis, *Collected Letters*, 1:268.

52. Lewis, *Collected Letters*, 1:268.

53. Lewis, *Collected Letters*, 1:269.

54. Lewis, *Collected Letters*, 1:271.

55. Lewis, *Collected Letters*, 1:272.

56. Lewis, *Collected Letters*, 1:270.

57. Lewis, *Collected Letters*, 1:282.

The descent continued and there are other comments directed at sexual proclivities that readers of these letters can decipher for themselves. Then, in a letter dated March 6, 1917, Lewis realizes that "something was wrong."[58] He tells Arthur that he had been reviewing an old letter from him that was "full of enthusiasm about books and music and scenery."[59] The contents of this old letter are more wholesome, and Lewis desires that their future discussions pertaining to sex be elevated. "Let us talk of these things when we want, but always keep them on the side that tends to beauty, and avoid everything that tends to sordid-ness and beastly police court sort of scandal out of grim real life like the O. Wilde story."[60] Lewis's reference is to Oscar Wilde, the Oxford-educated novelist and playwright who was convicted in 1885 in London of violating Section 11 of the Criminal Law Amendment Act, 1885, which made acts of gross indecency, particularly with men, a crime. This is an ominous reminder to his friend that certain sexual activity was still criminalized.[61] Lewis's appeal to "beauty" in future discussions with Arthur portends a significant shift in worldview, to be examined in the next chapter.

Many of us live with regret and embarrassment at things we did and said when we were adolescents. C. S. Lewis was no different. Later in his life, Lewis had the opportunity to expunge the evidence of this short-lived fixation with sadism. During the process of accumulating materials for Warnie's project on the history of the Lewis family, Lewis wrote Arthur in September of 1931, requesting that he return the letters from this period so that Warnie could include them in his project. Arthur returned them immediately and Lewis acknowledges their receipt in the very next letter. Reviewing the letters again, Lewis is "surprised" to find that a significant portion of their contents are centered around discussions pertaining to sex.[62] Instead of regretting that he and Arthur

---

58. Lewis, *Collected Letters*, 1:288.

59. Lewis, *Collected Letters*, 1:288.

60. Lewis, *Collected Letters*, 1:288.

61. Pearce, *Unmasking of Oscar Wilde*, 327.

62. Lewis, *Collected Letters*, 1:973.

had documented for posterity their thoughts on sensitive topics, Lewis is pleased "that we confided in each other . . . because it has done no harm in the long run – and how could adolescents really be friends without it?" One of the qualities of a deep friendship is the revelation, one to the other, of matters that are most private, and there is nothing more private than one's sexuality. This is a subject C. S. Lewis and Arthur Greeves would return to in the future. Instead, Lewis is most embarrassed by two other things in the letters from this period. The first is the "pretended assignation with the Belgian" girl. The second is that, as he looks back with the hindsight of an adult, he is struck by "their egotism: sometimes in the form of priggery, intellectual and even social: often in the form of downright affectation (I seem to be posturing and showing off in every letter)."[63]

Some of these letters never made their way to Warnie, especially the letters referencing sadism. Instead, Lewis "suppressed" them by returning them directly to Arthur. After Arthur's death in 1966, his cousin by marriage, Lisbeth Greeves, returned 225 letters from C. S. Lewis to Warnie Lewis.[64] It was Arthur's wish that these letters find their home at the University of Oxford's library. Warnie disregarded Arthur's wishes and sent them to Wheaton College. Later, in 1973, just after Warnie had died, Lisbeth Greeves sent Walter Hooper, who had become Lewis's trustee, another fifty letters from Lewis to Arthur. How sad that almost all the letters from Arthur to C. S. Lewis remain lost, probably forever.

Lewis's previously mentioned view of the world which came most naturally to him, expressed in *Surprised By Joy* as "'we two' or 'we few' (and in a sense 'we happy few') stand together against something stronger and larger,"[65] is reflected in these early letters to Arthur. Though they had been friends for just about three years, the sixty letters from Lewis to Arthur during this period and the unknown answers from Arthur to Lewis that are hinted at in Lewis's letters reveal two young men united together by a love of books,

63. Lewis, *Collected Letters*, 1:973.

64. Lewis, *They Stand Together*, 39.

65. Lewis, *Surprised by Joy*, 32.

reading, and music. Like all friends, they fought (and they would fight in the future), as Lewis's arrogance flared up toward Arthur in condescending comments from time to time. Yet there was always a reconciliation, exemplified in this comment from Lewis in a November 1916 letter: "what I do hope you will remember old man, that real friendships are very, very, rare and one doesn't want to endanger them by quarrelling over trifles. We always seem to be sparring now a days: I dare say its largely my fault (tho' in this case I really don't know why you're so angry) but anyway do let us stop it."[66] But, during this brief period of time, their love of the same things, coupled with an increasing vulnerability in revealing their innermost thoughts and secrets, served as a talisman against their encroaching adulthood and a dangerous world war.

---

66. Lewis, *Collected Letters*, 1:253.

CHAPTER 3

The Dry Tree

C. S. Lewis was wounded on April 15, 1918, during the Battle of Arras when an English shell exploded behind him. Lewis's 1st Battalion Somerset Light Infantry had been engaged with the Germans in the French village of Riez du Vinage since April 3.[1] In a letter to his father dated May 4, 1918, Lewis describes the extent of his injuries, writing, "As a matter of fact I was really hit in the back of the left hand, on the left leg from behind and just above the knee, and in the left side just under the arm pit. All three were only flesh wounds."[2] In a subsequent letter, he informs his father that his injuries are more serious than he had originally expressed, as "the one under my arm is worse than a flesh wound, as the bit of metal which went in there is now in my chest, high up under my 'pigeon chest' as shown: this however is nothing to worry about as it is doing no harm."[3] This piece of shrapnel would remain with Lewis for the remainder of his life.

As he spent time convalescing from his injuries at a military hospital in Etaples, France, Lewis began a revealing series of three letters with Arthur, in which we can observe the seeds that germinated and eventually flowered into a Christian faith that would ultimately be responsible for some of the greatest apologetic writing

1. Lewis, *Collected Letters*, 1:364.
2. Lewis, *Collected Letters*, 1:367.
3. Lewis, *Collected Letters*, 1:368.

of the last one hundred years. The main theme of these letters is "Beauty," which is remarkable considering Lewis had just left the trenches of the First World War, where he had undoubtedly witnessed terrible horrors, the very opposite of beauty.

In the first of these letters, dated May 23, 1918, Lewis alludes to some of these horrors, "shells, bullets, animal fears, animal pains,"[4] associating them to "the dominion of matter." Lewis devises an almost gnostic formula for his feelings about matter, "Matter = Nature =Satan," which he then contrasts with "Beauty, the only spiritual & not-natural thing I have yet found."[5] This idea of beauty must have been troubling for Lewis the atheist. For the atheist, there is no God and, as such, humanity resides in a closed universe—matter is all there is. But if beauty is "spiritual & not-natural," Lewis was hearing a tapping on the other side of the walls enclosing his materialistic worldview.

This letter closes with a "song" that would later appear in his first published book, *Spirits in Bondage*, a collection of poems published March 20, 1919 and composed between 1914 right up through his time on the front lines. The bulk of these poems were contained in a brown notebook he titled "The Metrical Meditations of a Cod."[6] The term "Cod" is an Ulster expression of "humorous and insincere self-depreciation." While Lewis was off fighting in the war, he entrusted the notebook to Arthur for safekeeping. Lewis writes Arthur that *Spirits in Bondage* is "mainly strung round the idea that I mentioned to you before – that nature is wholly diabolical & malevolent and that God, if he exists, is outside of and in opposition to the cosmic arrangements."[7] Still, there are hints within *Spirits in Bondage* that Lewis was flirting with something more than the numinous.

This "song" at the end of the first of the three letters on beauty wonders how "dead things/ be Half so lovely as they are?"[8] The

---

4. Lewis, *Collected Letters*, 1:371.

5. Lewis, *Collected Letters*, 1:371.

6. Hooper, *C. S. Lewis*, 139.

7. Lewis, *Collected Letters*, 1:379.

8. Lewis, *Collected Letters*, 1:372.

"wreathed star on star"[9] on a winter's night induces a "delight" and "desire" that fills our spirits. Because "Atoms dead could never thus/ Wake the human heart of us,"[10] there must be something, or Someone, who is the source of that beauty, delight, and desire. In the last five lines of the poem, Lewis tells us who that is:

> Unless the beauty that we see
> Part of endless beauty be,
> Thronged with spirits that have trod
> Where the bright foot-prints of God
> Lie fresh upon the heavenly sod.[11]

Lewis concludes this poem by stating God is the source of the beauty we see in the stars and on a winter's night. The God found in this poem is a very different from the God portrayed in the rest of *Spirits in Bondage*. The God in this poem has left his footprints upon the heavenly sod, evoking both delight and desire. Moving forward, desire would play a central role in Lewis's journey to faith.

Arthur must have responded to Lewis's thoughts on beauty, because in his next letter to Arthur, just six days later, he writes, "The thing in your last letter with which I most want to disagree is the remark about Beauty and nature."[12] In this letter, Lewis develops the idea from his previous letter and "song" that there must be something spiritual about beauty. Finding beauty in the color of a tree merely constitutes "sensations in my eye, produced by vibrations on the aether between me and the tree: the real tree is something quite different – a combination of colourless, shapeless, invisible atoms. It follows that neither the tree, nor any other material object can be beautiful in itself."[13] There must be more to beauty in that it cannot be merely the confluence of molecules and atoms that make up the physical material of a tree. It is just here where his materialistic bubble has been burst. "You see the

9. Lewis, *Collected Letters*, 1:372.
10. Lewis, *Collected Letters*, 1:373.
11. Lewis, *Collected Letters*, 1:373.
12. Lewis, *Collected Letters*, 1:374.
13. Lewis, *Collected Letters*, 1:374.

conviction is gaining ground on me that after all Spirit does exist . . . I fancy that there is Something right outside time & place, which did create matter as the Christians say."[14]

Not only does the beauty come from outside the material universe, but Lewis writes that beauty "is the call of the spirit in that something to the spirit in us."[15] Beauty is used as a signpost, or a pointer to something else. In concluding this letter's section on beauty, Lewis makes an important admission when he writes, "You see how frankly I admit that my views have changed."[16]

It is evident that within a week Arthur had responded. In the third and final letter dealing with beauty, Lewis picks up the discussion of their tree, "the Dry Tree as it might well be called from the nature of the discussions to which it gives rise."[17] In further developing the idea that beauty is not found within nature, he points out that if beauty were located within the tree, two people looking at that tree would see the exact same beauty. "But nothing is easier than to find two people one of whom would see beauty and the other see no beauty in the same tree."[18]

From this series of three letters, it is obvious that a significant change had occurred within Lewis. He was certainly in no immediate danger of becoming a Christian, as evidenced by the last paragraph of the third and final letter, where he writes, "I believe in no God, least of all in one that would punish me for the 'lusts of the flesh.'"[19] Yet Lewis now affirmatively recognized that there is something beyond matter and nature, a "universal spirit" where "all good & joyful things" are located, and that, more importantly, a part of this larger universal spirit resided in him.[20] It can be fairly stated that Lewis had now moved along the spiritual spectrum to a

---

14. Lewis, *Collected Letters*, 1:374.
15. Lewis, *Collected Letters*, 1:374.
16. Lewis, *Collected Letters*, 1:374.
17. Lewis, *Collected Letters*, 1:376.
18. Lewis, *Collected Letters*, 1:377.
19. Lewis, *Collected Letters*, 1:379.
20. Lewis, *Collected Letters*, 1:379.

form of theism. His spiritual antenna was up, and he was detecting signs of life from outside of what his eyes could see.

CHAPTER 4

"First Friends"

C. S. Lewis RETURNED to England on May 25th, 1918, and telegraphed his father that he was at Endsleigh Palace Hospital in London.[1] Five days later he wrote his father, asking for a visit and for some clothes.[2] While Albert Lewis did not make it to see his son, Lewis did have a frequent visitor as he convalesced. Mrs. Janie Moore was the mother of Lewis's roommate, Edward "Paddy" Moore. Lewis and Moore were billeted together during their military training at Keeble College. Janie and her other child, Maureen, age twelve, desired to remain close to Paddy for as long as possible, so she rented rooms near Oxford. Lewis first mentions Paddy in a letter to Arthur from June 10, 1917, describing him as "quite a good fellow too, tho' a little too childish and virtuous for 'common nature's daily food.'"[3] It was right around this period that Lewis met Janie Moore for the very first time.

The fact that Lewis was rooming with Paddy necessitated further interaction with Mrs. Moore. One week after the letter to Arthur referring to Paddy, Lewis wrote to his father and included passing comments about the Moore family, with Paddy being "a very decent sort of man; his mother, an Irish lady, is staying up

1. Lewis, *Collected Letters*, 1:373.
2. Lewis, *Collected Letters*, 1:376.
3. Lewis, *Collected Letters*, 1:319.

here and I have met her once or twice."[4] In August, Lewis spent a week with the Moores in their home in Oxford. He informed his father of his week with the Moores in an August 17 letter that includes a reference to Mrs. Moore: "I like her immensely."[5] Just a few weeks later, Lewis spent three weeks of his four-week leave with the Moores; as mentioned in the previous chapter, this was a contributing factor to the dysfunction in the relationship between Lewis and his father. At some point during these three weeks with the Moores, Lewis and Paddy promised each other that if one of them survived and the other did not, the survivor would look after the other's parent.[6]

Sadly, Paddy Moore was reported missing in action on March 24, 1918, during the battle at Pargny, France. In a letter to Mrs. Moore, the adjutant of his battalion wrote, "I have to tell you that your very gallant son was reported missing on the 24th of last month. He was last seen on the morning of that day with a few men defending a position on a river bank against infinitely superior numbers of the enemy. All the other officers and most of the men of his company have become casualties, and I fear it is impossible to obtain more definite information . . . We all feel his loss very deeply, and I cannot express too strongly our sympathy with you."[7] While Mrs. Moore suspected her son's death, it wasn't until September that Paddy was confirmed to be deceased.

It was also toward the end of that extended four-week leave from mid-August to mid-September 1917, when Lewis returned home to spend the last week with his father, that he most likely confided to Arthur his feelings for Mrs. Moore. Later that month, in a letter to Arthur dated October 28, we see a veiled reference to this conversation. Lewis begins the letter, "Since coming back & meeting a certain person I have begun to realize that it was not at all the right thing for me to tell you so much as I did. I must therefore try to undo my actions as far as possible by asking you

4. Lewis, *Collected Letters*, 1:322.

5. Lewis, *Collected Letters*, 1:334.

6. Lewis, *Collected Letters*, 1:2021.

7. Lewis, *Collected Letters*, 1:369–70.

& try to forget my various statements & not to refer to the subject. Of course I have perfect trust in you, mon vieux, but still I have no business to go discussing those sort of things with you. So in future that topic must be taboo between us."[8]

When C. S. Lewis met Janie Moore, she was forty-five years old. He was eighteen. She married Courtney Edward Moore in 1897.[9] Though they never divorced, Janie left her husband in 1907, taking the two children with her.[10] While we will never know for certain whether their relationship in their early years together was romantic, Walter Hooper, Lewis's Boswell, concludes that it is "not improbable" that there was a sexual component to their relationship before Lewis's conversion to Christianity.[11] Similarly, George Sayer, who was a student and close friend of Lewis, and who wrote what Walter Hooper calls the "standard" biography of Lewis, initially dismissed the idea of a sexual componant to their relationship, but in later editions of his Lewis biography acknowledged that that he was "quite certain" they were sexually intimate.[12]

What is certain is that, while he was somewhat transient during his recovery from his wounds, each time Lewis changed his locus, he was situated physically near Janie Moore. Shortly after his return to England in late May of 1918, Lewis was sent to recover at Ashton Court, in Clifton, Bristol, on June 25, which was close to Mrs. Moore's home at the time.[13] From Bristol, Lewis was then sent on October 4 to the convalescence camp Perham Downs in Ludgershall, which Lewis described as "a place much cursed by most army people who are sent there because it is in the heart of the country and cannot therefore afford them the only pleasures of which they are capable."[14] Janie Moore subsequently took a cot-

---

8. Lewis, *Collected Letters*, 1:339.

9. Lewis, *Collected Letters*, 1:1020.

10. Lewis, *Collected Letters*, 1:1020.

11. Lewis, *Collected Letters*, 1:2022.

12. Sayer, *Jack*, xvii.

13. Lewis, *They Stand Together*, 225.

14. Lewis, *Collected Letters*, 1:403.

tage nearby.[15] On November 11, Lewis was sent to Eastbourne, near the southwestern tip of England. Once again, Janie Moore moved to be near Lewis.[16] Lewis's convalescence odyssey finally ended on Christmas Eve, 1918, when he was discharged from care and demobilized from the army.[17]

In addition to Lewis's disclosure to Arthur about a "certain person," there are other clues contained in his correspondence with Arthur pointing to an evolving and deepening attachment with Mrs. Moore. Just two weeks after arriving on the front lines at the end of November, 1917, Lewis starts his letter to Arthur by thanking him for writing to Mrs. Moore, telling him "how nice & homely it is for me to know that the two people who matter most to me in the world are in touch."[18] A few weeks later, in a letter dated February 2, 1918, he writes of longing for "one of our old afternoons again when we sat in your drawing room and discussed our tea," and of "real walks far away in the hills."[19] Perhaps worrying that those days are gone, he assures Arthur, and also perhaps himself, that he wants to return to those times and that he will have the margin in his life to do so because "after all there is room for other things besides love in a man's life."[20] For emphasis, Lewis follows up with the statement, "As well, you should trust in me after I have given you so much confidence."[21] His very next letter to Arthur continues the nostalgic theme of their friendship. Lewis wistfully considers whether he and Arthur will ever see each other again while remembering their rain-soaked walks and Loki-inspired opera. Ultimately, he remains optimistic that "good times" for he and Arthur remain ahead, "although I have been at a war and although I love someone."[22]

15. McGrath, *C. S. Lewis*, 76.

16. McGrath, *C. S. Lewis*, 76.

17. Lewis, *Collected Letters*, 1:423.

18. Lewis, *Collected Letters*, 1:348.

19. Lewis, *Collected Letters*, 1:353.

20. Lewis, *Collected Letters*, 1:353.

21. Lewis, *Collected Letters*, 1:353.

22. Lewis, *Collected Letters*, 1:355.

It wasn't just Arthur who was observing in real time the flowering of the relationship between Lewis and Mrs. Moore. In a letter to his father dated May 10, 1919, Lewis's brother, Warnie, expressed his consternation by commenting, "The whole thing irritates me by its freakishness."[23] Lewis's father replied with his own concerns: "It worries and depresses me greatly. All I know about the lady is that she is old enough to be his mother . . . If Jacks were not an impetuous, kind-hearted creature who could be cajoled by any woman who has been through the mill, I should not be so uneasy. Then there is the husband whom I have always been told is a scoundrel."[24]

The fact that there is still no absolute certainty regarding the status of the relationship between C. S. Lewis and Janie Moore is a testimony to Lewis's efforts at misdirection and subterfuge. Yet there is evidence that some form of a relationship existed between the two and the existing evidence at least rises to the level of a preponderance. In the introduction for Lewis's published diary from 1922–1927 titled *All My Road Before Me*, Walter Hooper writes that the two had "motive, means, and opportunity."[25] The contents of Lewis's letters from this period invite the conclusion of a reciprocal romantic attachment. First, there is the letter composed just after spending three weeks with the Moore family, where Lewis writes to Arthur of a "certain person" and asks him to forget their discussion regarding that person. Then, after Lewis's arrival at the front, there is a compilation of references over the next few letters that include naming Mrs. Moore as one of the two people who mean the most to Lewis, and two separate allusions to Lewis being in love with someone. As he had done since the very first letter from Jack in 1914, now penned almost four years earlier, Arthur Greeves continued to serve as the repository for Jack Lewis's secrets.

After being demobilized from the military on Christmas Eve 1918, and then spending some time with his father and brother at

23. Hooper, *C. S. Lewis*, 12.

24. Lewis, *Collected Letters*, 1:451.

25. Lewis, *All My Roads Before Me*, 9.

home in Belfast, Lewis returned to Oxford to resume his studies on January 13, 1919. He did not return alone. Mrs. Moore and Maureen also came to Oxford with him. Until they took up residence in their permanent home, commonly known as the Kilns, in 1930, Lewis, Janie Moore, and Maureen resided together in nine different locations between 1917 and 1930.[26] Their transient lifestyle was the result of their lack of money. The average cost associated with attending Oxford at that time was approximately sixty British pounds per term with one pound valued at five US dollars at the time.[27] Lewis's scholarship provided him with eighty pounds for the term. That did not leave him much left over. Fortunately, Lewis's father provided him with another sixty-seven pounds per term as an allowance. In addition, Lewis received 145 pounds in March of 1919 and another 104 pounds in July as a wounds gratuity from his injuries suffered during the war.[28] This should have been sufficient for a single male student to live on, but Lewis was not living as a single student.

In a January 26, 1919, letter to Arthur detailing his life at Oxford, Lewis tells Arthur that Mrs. Moore is "installed in our 'own hired house' (like St Paul only not daily preaching and teaching)."[29] This line is a reference to Luke's description of a period of Paul's life in Acts 28:30: "He lived there two whole years at his own expense, and welcomed all who came to him."[30] In his very next letter to Arthur two weeks later, Lewis refers to Janie and Maureen as "The family."[31] Lewis had shown them a picture of Arthur and "they didn't expect you to be so good-looking! & Mrs Moore asks me to ask you for one for herself and sends her love."[32] That Lewis was still cloaking his relationship with Janie Moore from his father is

---

26. Lewis, *All My Roads Before Me*, 7.

27. Lewis, *All My Roads Before Me*, 6.

28. Lewis, *All My Roads Before Me*, 6.

29. Lewis, *Collected Letters*, 1:425.

30. Acts 28:30.

31. Lewis, *Collected Letters*, 1:433.

32. Lewis, *Collected Letters*, 1:433.

evidenced from the letter's postscript: "P.S. Nearly all of this is fit for 'publication' except one sentence."[33]

Up to this point in his life, the significant and deep male friendships experienced by Lewis had been limited to Arthur and his brother, Warnie. His return to his studies at Oxford exposed him to a large segment of other men who were not unlike himself: young, bright, gifted, intellectually curious, and having just survived the savagery of the First World War. This provided him with the opportunity to expand and enlarge his circle of friends, with many of these new acquaintances developing into some of his closest lifelong friends.

The first lifelong friend Lewis met at Oxford was A. K. Hamilton Jenkin. It is interesting to note that sometimes when Lewis described one friend, he used Arthur Greeves to illuminate the reference to the friend he was discussing. Lewis does this when describing Jenkin in *Surprised by Joy*, writing that Jenkin "continues (what Arthur had begun) my education as a seeing, listening, smelling, receptive creature."[34] Jenkin and Lewis shared bike rides and Jenkin often visited Lewis and Mrs. Moore at their home.

Shortly thereafter, Lewis met Owen Barfield in the fall of 1919, and their friendship blossomed. In *Surprised by Joy*, Lewis again compares and contrasts his friendship with another to Arthur. Lewis calls Arthur a "First Friend" and Barfield a "Second Friend."[35] As a "First Friend," Lewis describes Arthur as an "alter ego, the man who first reveals to you that you are not alone in the world" because he shares "all your most secret delights."[36] That feeling of not being alone in the world, which defines a "First Friend" for Lewis, can be traced back to that pivotal moment in Arthur's room when he saw Arthur with a copy of *Myths of the Norsemen* and realized that there was someone else who liked the very same things he did.

---

33. Lewis, *Collected Letters*, 1:433.
34. Lewis, *Surprised by Joy*, 199.
35. Lewis, *Surprised by Joy*, 199.
36. Lewis, *Surprised by Joy*, 199.

Conversely, a "Second Friend" is someone who shares your interests, yet "disagrees with you about everything."[37] These disagreements lead to a combativeness within the friendship, with "each learning the weight of the other's punches, and often more like mutually respectful enemies than friends."[38] This combativeness between Lewis and Barfield began when Barfield (and another of Lewis's lifelong friends, Cecil Harwood) began to subscribe to the belief system known as Anthroposophy. Anthroposophy originated with the Austrian philosopher Rudolf Steiner and claimed that human beings can access divine wisdom on their own power. For Lewis, Barfield's acceptance of anthroposophy "marked the beginning of what I can only describe as the Great War between him and me."[39] This "Great War" between the two is memorialized in a series of letters most likely written in the years 1927 and 1928. There were perhaps many letters between the two, but only ten letters remain from Lewis's pen and two from Barfield's, though they are only drafts of the originals he mailed to Lewis.[40] It is certainly safe to assume that, in addition to the "Great War" letters, Lewis and Barfield discussed Barfield's (and Harwood's) devotion to anthroposophy on walks, at each other's home's (Barfield and Harwood shared a cottage together), and at school. Barfield resided in or near Oxford until 1929, affording he and Lewis ample opportunity to spend time together before Barfield moved to London in 1929 to practice law with his father.

While many of Barfield's thoughts seemed antipodean to Lewis's, their discussion never exceeded a certain level of hostility. Lewis never qualifies his conversations with Barfield as "a quarrel." Instead, Lewis describes his disagreements with Barfield as "an almost incessant disputation, sometimes by letter and sometimes face to face, which lasted for years."[41] Barfield's commitment to

---

37. Lewis, *Surprised by Joy*, 199.

38. Lewis, *Surprised by Joy*, 200.

39. Lewis, *Surprised by Joy*, 207.

40. Lewis, *Collected Letters*, 1:1598.

41. Lewis, *Surprised by Joy*, 207.

anthroposophy cooled later in his life as he was baptized in the Church of England in 1949.[42]

Out of the friction between the two, a respect and admiration grew. Lewis later admits that his tussles with Barfield had changed him more than he had changed Barfield, with one of those changes resulting in the elimination of Lewis's "chronological snobbery."[43] Lewis's "chronological snobbery" when he met Barfield refers to Lewis's belief that the intellectual orthodoxy of the current period was superior to preceding periods in history. In his preface to *The Allegory of Love*, published in 1936, Lewis writes that it is Barfield who "has taught me not to patronize the past, and has trained me to see the present as itself a 'period.'"[44] In a testament to his affection and respect for Barfield, Lewis dedicates *The Allegory of Love* to him, writing, "To Owen Barfield Wisest and best of my unofficial teachers." Barfield later reciprocated by dedicating one of his books, *Poetic Diction: A Study in Meaning*, to Lewis with, "To C. S. Lewis 'Opposition is true friendship.'"

Lewis's friendship with Barfield led him to another lifelong friend, Cecil Harwood. Barfield and Harwood had known each other from their time together at Highgate School when they were each just twelve years old. It was through Cecil Harwood that the root of anthroposophy popped up into the Lewis-Barfield-Harwood triumvirate. In 1922, Harwood met Daphne Oliver at an English Folk Dance Society event.[45] The future Mrs. Harwood was a teacher and in the same year she met Cecil she attended a Rudolf Steiner lecture.[46] She would go on to assist in establishing a school devoted to the teachings of anthroposophy in London. Eventually, she brought Cecil and Owen Barfield to one of Steiner's lectures. In an entry to his diary dated July 7, 1923, Lewis records that he and Harwood were finishing tea under the tress on his lawn when Harwood "told me of this new philosopher, Rudolf Steiner, who

42. Lewis, *Collected Letters*, 1:981.

43. Lewis, *Surprised by Joy*, 207.

44. Lewis, *Allegory of Love*, x.

45. Lewis, *Collected Letters*, 1:998.

46. Lewis, *Collected Letters*, 1:998.

has, 'made the burden role from my back.'"[47] Lewis expressed his disappointment to Harwood with this development, yet it would not serve as a barrier to their existing and deepening friendship. Throughout his life, Lewis had an affinity for long walks in the countryside with his friends, and Harwood was a regular participant. This led to Lewis nicknaming him "Lord of the Walks."[48] As he had done with Owen Barfield with the *Allegory of Love*, as a tribute to his friendship Lewis dedicated his book *Miracles*, published in 1947, to Cecil and Daphne Harwood. Lewis's friendships with Barfield and Harwood each had a different flavor. In a letter to Jenkin, Lewis writes that one of the benefits of being Barfield's friend is that he has derived "sheer wisdom and a sort of richness of spirit" from Barfield, while he goes to Harwood for "humours" and the appreciation of them.[49]

Another of his lifelong friendships forged early in his time at Oxford was with Nevil Coghill. Coghill first appears in Lewis's diary on February 2, 1922, where he describes Coghill as "an enthusiastic sensible man, without nonsense, and a gentleman, much more attractive than the majority."[50] When they first met, in a class taught by George Gordon in the Michaelmas term of 1922, Lewis was surprised that Coghill, "clearly the most intelligent and best-informed man in that class," was a Christian and took his faith seriously.[51] Coghill's first recollection of Lewis was from that class as well. He remembered Lewis reading a paper for the class on *The Faerie Queen*. "Lewis seemed to carry the class with him in his combative pleasure; his paper made a strong effect. It was certainly the best the class had heard."[52] In June of 1923, both Lewis and Coghill received First Class Honours in English, among only six students earning this honor.

47. Lewis, *All My Roads Before Me*, 254.

48. Lewis, *Collected Letters*, 1:998.

49. Lewis, *Collected Letters*, 1:653.

50. Lewis, *All My Roads Before Me*, 189.

51. Lewis, *Surprised by Joy*, 212

52. In Gibb, ed., *Light on Lewis*, 52.

The First in English meant that Lewis was now the owner of the academic distinction of a "Triple First," having earned a First in Classical Honour Moderations in 1920 and another First in "Greats" in 1922. But even with this impressive resume he struggled to find employment. By the middle of 1924, the unemployed Lewis received a one-year temporary fellowship teaching philosophy. The pay was minimal, so Lewis supplemented his income by tutoring other students. During the spring of 1925, a fellowship opened at Magdalen College to teach English. English as a subject was a growth sector for Oxford in the early 1920s and perhaps Lewis's decision to pursue a course of study in English in 1923 was accompanied with the thought that there may be a future for him in the growing English department. As Lewis was pursuing the position, he learned that his friend Nevil Coghill was also a candidate for the position.[53] Eventually, Coghill withdrew so he could accept a fellowship at his own college, Exeter.

On May 25, 1925, Albert Lewis received a telephone call from the local post office informing him that a telegram had arrived for him. He told the person on the other end to read it to him and Albert heard the words, "Elected Fellow Magdalen. Jack."[54] Albert recorded in his diary that he next went to his room "and burst into tears of joy. I knelt down and thanked God with a full heart. My prayers had been heard and answered."[55] Fellow and tutor in English language and literature would be a position C. S. Lewis would hold for the next twenty-nine years.

Lewis records in his diary that it was through his duties as a faculty member that he first met J. R. R. Tolkien. This first meeting occurred at a tea in conjunction with a faculty meeting on May 11, 1926. Lewis describes Tolkien as "a smooth, pale, fluent little chap" and that there is, "No harm in him: only needs a smack or so."[56] The friendship between Lewis and Tolkien was incredibly consequential. There was a reciprocal element to it in that it was Lewis

---

53. Lewis, *Collected Letters*, 1:643.
54. Lewis, *Collected Letters*, 1:642.
55. Lewis, *Collected Letters*, 1:642.
56. Lewis, *All My Roads Before Me*, 393.

who encouraged and spurred Tolkien on to finish his magisterial *Lord of the Rings* while it was Tolkien who encouraged and spurred Lewis on in Lewis's journey to Christianity.

The same year Lewis and Tolkien became acquainted, Tolkien started an informal group called the "Kolbitars," a precursor to the more famous group known as the "Inklings." Lewis writes Arthur about the group, describing it as "a little Icelandic Club in Oxford called the 'Kolbitar': which means (literally) 'coal-biters', i.e. an Icelandic word for old cronies who sit around the fire so close that they look as if they were biting the coals."[57] Within a few years, Tolkien would be elevated to the level of a second-class friend, not in the sense Lewis used the term "Second Friend" in *Surprised By Joy*, whereby he and Barfield were constantly disagreeing about issues. Instead, in a September 22, 1931, letter to Arthur, Lewis uses the qualification "friends of the 2nd class" as a measure of the degree of affection or closeness Lewis felt to Tolkien.[58]

As the number and quality of Lewis's new friends grew at Oxford, it appears Arthur was trying to determine his own path in life. He must have presented his ideas concerning his future to Lewis early in 1920. In a letter from April of that year, Lewis gives Arthur his thoughts on the issue. First, he counsels Arthur that, whatever he does, he should leave Belfast, and all of Ireland. While affirming his own love for his native land, Lewis expresses that the staleness of familiar surroundings provides a heaviness that can serve as a drag on one's efforts. Arthur apparently had also considered attending Oxford, or at least moving there. While Lewis says this would "please" him, he cautions Arthur that "I could not see you so often nor so regularly as at home."[59] Lewis believed Arthur's best option was going to the Slade School of Fine Art in London. One does not have to read too deeply between the lines of Lewis's letter to sense the tinge of apprehension and uncertainty Arthur was struggling with in trying to find a purpose. Lewis tries to sooth his friend by telling him, "I still think it most unlikely that

---

57. Lewis, *Collected Letters*, 1:701.
58. Lewis, *Collected Letters*, 1:969.
59. Lewis, *Collected Letters*, 1:481.

all the romance and imagination which are in you should evapo-
rate in nothing more than appreciation of other people's work."[60]

The Slade School of Fine Art in London was the path Arthur
ultimately chose, enrolling there in January 1921 and remaining
until December of 1923. It is here that a large gap appears in their
correspondence, with only three letters between June of 1920 and
December of 1926. There are three possible explanations for this.
Walter Hooper suggests that Arthur may have lost some of the
letters from this period.[61] Another possible explanation is that
with Arthur's close proximity in London they saw each other more
frequently and had less use for written correspondence. The final
reason for their decreasing correspondence may have been Lewis's
growing relationships with his new friends at Oxford. The reality
may be that it was a combination of all three.

Arthur joined Lewis and the Moores for an extended visit
from June 28 through July 19, 1922. There is an old saying attributed to Benjamin Franklin that visitors, like fish, begin to smell
bad after three days. Franklin's pronouncement is reflected in
Lewis's recollection of this visit in his diary. On the very first day of
Arthur's arrival, Lewis writes, "Arthur is tremendously improved:
nearly all the nonsense is gone and he talked interestingly."[62]
While the visit started out on the right foot, it is apparent that
toward its conclusion Arthur had worn out his welcome. On the
day before he left, dinner was going to be later than expected because the mushroom stew being prepared wasn't quite ready. Lewis
made a comment about his father's habit of being annoyed if a
meal wasn't ready on time, to which Arthur replied, "Oh but some
people really do get sick if they don't have their meals at regular
times. Mother does. I'm just the same! So we gave him bread and
butter and he struggled on somehow."[63] This reference to Arthur's
mother triggered Lewis's memory of a comment Arthur had made
a few days earlier. It seems Lewis had had enough of Arthur's table

60. Lewis, *Collected Letters*, 1:483.
61. Lewis, *They Stand Together*, 285.
62. Lewis, *All My Roads Before Me*, 57.
63. Lewis, *Collected Letters*, 1:73.

etiquette and he "ventured to say something about the sucking, squeaking, crunching noises he makes in eating, from which D (Lewis's shorthand reference to Janie Moore in his diary) and I suffer tortures," to which Arthur replied, "I know. Sorry. It's in the family. Mother does it too."[64] To punctuate Arthur's visit, Lewis records that Arthur "departed with many and I think true regrets: I accompanied him in his taxi to the station."[65]

All was soon forgotten. Just six days later Lewis responds to a letter from Arthur and he bookends the letter by telling Arthur at the beginning how much he is missed and concluding the letter with the wish that Arthur will return soon.[66] Lewis got his wish the following summer when Arthur came for a two-week visit. It only took a few hours for the conditions of this visit to deteriorate. On the way home from picking Arthur up at the station they "renewed our earlier youths and laughed together like two schoolgirls."[67] By the end of the day Lewis was lamenting having to listen to Arthur's adventures since last Christmas. There is one long, protracted entry in Lewis's diary dated July 13–25, with the majority of it devoted to Arthur. Lewis writes that Arthur "is greatly changed."[68] Arthur stayed in his pajamas until noon and he further repulsed Lewis by "taking off his slippers in the dining room and laying his bare feet on the table. His feet are very long and he perspires freely."[69]

In this extended entry, Lewis mentions that he had introduced Arthur to an acquaintance from school. After the acquaintance had left, Arthur mentioned that he hoped the man would invite him to play tennis next day. In considering Arthur's wish, Lewis records, "I devoutly hoped he would not meet Thring again, as I hardly knew the man myself and did not want him exposed

---

64. Lewis, *Collected Letters*, 1:73.

65. Lewis, *All My Roads Before Me*, 73.

66. Lewis, *Collected Letters*, 1:596–97.

67. Lewis, *All My Roads Before Me*, 256.

68. Lewis, *All My Roads Before Me*, 257.

69. Lewis, *All My Roads Before Me*, 258.

to such naked cadging."[70] There are other instances in Lewis's diary where he appears to have been embarrassed both by and for Arthur in front of his Oxford friends.

A significant observation made by Lewis from this visit is a change in Arthur's "nature." "Someone has put it into his head the idea of being himself."[71] Lewis had become concerned with Arthur's new worldview as it had appeared to become untethered from at least one of the foundational tenets of the Christian faith, the belief in hell. For Arthur, the chief duty of man toward others was to merely be kind while the duty owed to himself was now "to swim with the tide and obey his desires."[72] It is interesting that Lewis, while not yet a Christian himself, would be concerned for his friend's departure from a faith that was at one point especially important to Arthur.

The undulation in their friendship during the 1920s concluded with Arthur's role as a companion during the days leading up to the death of Lewis's father, Albert. In July of 1929, several members of Albert Lewis's family were concerned with his appearance. At their urging, Albert sought medical attention. His diary entries from the last part of the month indicate he had been dealing with terrible pain, and a resulting x-ray occasioned this entry: "Result rather disquieting."[73] On the same day, Lewis writes to Arthur telling him that he's received word from several family members expressing their concern for his father. Lewis selfishly complains that this "bad news from home" will cramp his style when he returns to Ireland to visit, and that he will have to spend more time with his father than he wants.[74] He even envisions a worst-case scenario whereby his father's health deteriorates to a point where he will have to bring him back to Oxford, causing an unbearable disruption to the life Lewis had covertly built, "with God knows

---

70. Lewis, *All My Roads Before Me*, 258.

71. Lewis, *All My Roads Before Me*, 257.

72. Lewis, *All My Roads Before Me*, 257.

73. Lewis, *Collected Letters*, 1:804.

74. Lewis, *Collected Letters*, 1:805.

what upsets & difficulties for everyone I care about – you, Minto, Warnie, myself, everyone."[75]

In addition to self-centeredness, this letter also expresses an unflattering sentiment from Lewis. Before he even saw his father, he was concerned that he would have to feign love for him all the while rendering him "help & sympathy." He also includes the other startling revelation that he doesn't even like his father. Caring for a parent one holds in contempt and enmity would be a shared experience for he and Arthur, as Lewis reminds Arthur of his emotional experience at the death of his father over four years ago. Lewis arrived home the second week of August and became the primary caretaker for his father.[76] Caring for his father didn't seem to change Lewis's feelings for him, as Lewis makes clear in a September 9 letter to Owen Barfield. He informs Barfield, "1. I am attending at the almost sickbed of one for whom I have little affection and whose society has for many years given me much discomfort and no pleasure. 2. Nevertheless I find it almost unendurable."[77]

After some weeks, it was thought that Albert Lewis's condition had stabilized and that, though the diagnosis was cancer, specifically a carcinoma of the colon, the prognosis was that the cancer would progress slowly and he would live for several more years. Lewis returned to Oxford on September 22 to resume his teaching duties. Early on September 24, he was notified via telegram that his father's condition had taken a turn for the worse. Despite Jack leaving immediately to return to his father, Albert Lewis died the following day of cardiac arrest before his son could reach him.

Lewis's thoughts regarding his father during Albert Lewis's last days seem unduly harsh considering the financial generosity provided by Albert over the previous ten years. As time passed, Lewis was able to look back in hindsight and realize how poorly he had treated is father. Later in his life, Lewis had a running

75. Lewis, *Collected Letters*, 1:805.
76. Lewis, *They Stand Together*, 306.
77. Lewis, *Collected Letters*, 1:820.

correspondence with a woman named Rhona Bodle. In 1954, she wrote Lewis regarding problems she had in her relationship with her father. Lewis begins his response back with, "Oh how you touch my conscience! I treated my own father abominably and no sin in my whole life now seems to be so serious. It is not likely you are equally guilty."[78]

Caring for an ailing parent can be physically and emotionally exhausting. C. S. Lewis's experience of caring for his father was no different. Lewis reports to Owen Barfield that during this period he was refreshed at least once a day and sometimes twice a day by visits with Arthur. Under the stress of caring for his father, Lewis tells Barfield that his late-night conversations with Arthur consist of "a magical feeling of successful conspiracy: it is such a breach, not of course of the formal rules, but of the immemorial custom of a house where I have hardly ever known freedom."[79] It is under the crucible of caring for his father that Lewis and Greeves resolidified their friendship after a distancing earlier in the decade.

78. Lewis, *Collected Letters*, 3:445.

79. Lewis, *Collected Letters*, 1:821.

CHAPTER 5

Addison's Walk

WHILE MUCH HAS BEEN written on the subject of C. S. Lewis's conversion to Christianity, including his own account in the autobiographical *Surprised by Joy*, the pivot point for Lewis's conversion can be observed in real time through his correspondence with Arthur Greeves. These letters, specifically three between September 22 and October 18, 1931, are in one sense the culmination of Lewis's faith journey, and in another sense just the very beginning. Each of the three either detail or reference the fateful evening of September 19 on the hauntingly beautiful pathway Addison's Walk, located on the grounds of Magdalen College, where Lewis spent much of the evening speaking with J. R. R. Tolkien and Hugo Dyson about Christianity.

In thinking of these letters as the culmination of Lewis's journey, it becomes necessary to go back to the point where he took his first step. Lewis describes in *Surprised by Joy* an experience early in his life that produced "enormous bliss" when his brother Warnie brought his toy garden, which consisted of "a biscuit tin filled with moss," into their nursery.[1] This toy garden produced in Lewis a "sensation" of desire, "but desire for what?"[2] This intense desire evolved into longing, more specifically, "a longing for a longing,"[3]

1. Lewis, *Surprised by Joy*, 16.
2. Lewis, *Surprised by Joy*, 16.
3. Lewis, *Surprised by Joy*, 16.

and these two prongs, desire and longing, compelled Lewis along his spiritual trajectory. Lewis even has a name for this intense longing produced by desire, calling it "Joy." Specifically, "Joy is an unsatisfied desire which itself is more desirable than any other satisfaction."[4]

The concept of "Joy" bookends *Surprised by Joy*. Lewis defines the term early on and then concludes with the book's final paragraph telling readers that Joy is really what his story has been about. Much of Lewis's life had been in pursuit of that which would fulfill his desires and longings. Admittedly, Lewis writes in *Surprised by Joy*, he had sought fulfillment in the erotic, the occult, in music, in poetry, and all had left him empty.[5] It is a contemporary crisis as well, with many people thinking, "If I just get the next house, then I'll be happy," or, "If I can get the next job, or the next spouse, then I will really be happy."

Lewis uses a walk he took as a young adult to illustrate this point. He recollects the beauty of his surroundings, the morning's white mist, "the drops of moisture on every branch," the coldness of the hillside, and the distant sounds from the local town.[6] His father had just sent him several volumes of Wagner's *The Ring of the Nibelung*, which he had been looking forward to reading with great anticipation. The confluence of the beauty of the surroundings and the excitement of his new reading material "produced a longing" whereby Lewis felt that he "had tasted heaven then."[7] Even the memory of that walk evoked within him similar feelings. Alas, Lewis realizes that these desires and longings have no corresponding possession attached to them. The only thing we are able to possess is the feeling of longing or desire itself. Joy, that "unsatisfied desire which itself is more desirable than any other satisfaction," is really then a signpost to something, or Someone, else. This sentiment is captured in one of C. S. Lewis's most famous quotes, which is found in *Mere Christianity*: "If I find in myself

4. Lewis, *Surprised by Joy*, 17–18.
5. Lewis, *Surprised by Joy*, 169.
6. Lewis, *Surprised by Joy*, 166.
7. Lewis, *Surprised by Joy*, 166.

desires which nothing in this world can satisfy, the only logical explanation is that I was made for another world."[8]

When Lewis writes in that final paragraph in *Surprised by Joy* that the subject of Joy has "lost nearly all interest for me since I became a Christian,"[9] it is from the other side of the divide that separates belief in Christianity from unbelief. He had come to the realization that all followers of Christ must eventually come to: it is only Christ who satisfies all our deepest desires and longings. St. Augustine rightly concluded that our fallen human hearts are restless until we rest in God.

Wrestling with desire and longing, and the accompanying sense of Joy they produced, was only one number in the combination required to unlock the padlock that secured Lewis's unbelief. Lewis had been intellectually formed during his school days at Bookham by William Kirkpatrick, "The Great Knock." This meant that Lewis had been rigorously trained to considered any and all intellectual propositions in the cold, unrefracted light of logic and reason. In a talk given to a pacifist organization in 1940, titled "Why I Am Not a Pacifist," Lewis provides an exposition on the three-part intellectual formula that reason requires.[10] First, one must receive the facts regarding the proposition under consideration, the majority of which will be supplied from sources other than ourselves. Second, one must use their "intuition" to derive self-evident truths about these facts. Finally, one must employ "an art or skill of arranging the facts so as to yield a series of such intuitions that, linked together, produce a proof of the truth or falsehood" of the proposition under consideration.

It is through this careful grid of reason and logic that Lewis would consider the truth or falsehood of Christianity, and, like almost all the other major and important events in his life, it is through his letters to Arthur that Lewis records this process in real time. Much like the trilogy of three letters to Arthur regarding "The Dry Tree," where Lewis had come to the realization there was

8. Lewis, *Mere Christianity*, 136.

9. Lewis, *Surprised by Joy*, 238.

10. Lewis *Weight of Glory*, 65–66

something outside his materialistic worldview, he now chronicled the climax of his conversion to Christianity in another trilogy of letters to Arthur in the fall of 1931.

Two intermediaries accompanied Lewis along this final leg of his journey to Christianity and their roles are highlighted in these three letters. The first was J. R. R. Tolkien. The Lewis-Tolkien friendship had deepened since that first faculty meeting where Lewis felt a "smack or so" was the only thing Tolkien needed. His early relationship with Tolkien enabled him to overcome two pre-existing prejudices: not trusting Catholics, and not trusting philologists.[11] The other individual present that evening was Hugo Dyson. Lewis had become acquainted with Dyson within the last year, having been introduced to him through Nevil Coghill. When they met, Dyson was a lecturer and tutor at the University of Reading. Lewis wrote Arthur about one of their first meetings at the end of July 1930. Dyson had been visiting at Oxford and spent the night with Lewis, and the two stayed up until three in the morning talking. Lewis desired to accelerate their friendship, telling Arthur, "My feeling was apparently reciprocated and I think we sat up so late with the feeling that heaven knew when we might meet again and the new friendship had to be freed past its youth into maturity in a single evening."[12] By the time Dyson played his important role along with Tolkien on the night of September 19, 1931, at Addison's Walk, and later that evening at Lewis's room, Dyson had been promoted by Lewis to a friend "of the 2nd class – i.e. not in the same rank as yourself and Barfield, but on a level with Tolkien or Macfarlane."[13]

In the first of these three letters to Arthur describing the pivot point of Lewis's faith journey, the scene is set. Addison's Walk is a picturesque and popular walking path located on the grounds Magdalen College. It was there that Dyson, Lewis, and Tolkien headed after dinner. Lewis writes that during their walk they discussed the meaning of metaphor and myth. While they

---

11. Lewis, *Surprised by Joy*, 216.
12. Lewis, *Collected Letters*, 1:918.
13. Lewis, *Collected Letters*, 1:969.

were walking along and talking, Lewis records, the three were, "interrupted by a rush of wind which came so suddenly on the still, warm evening and sent so many leaves pattering down that we thought it was raining."[14] Tolkien and Dyson, Lewis writes, appreciated the ecstasy of the moment, perhaps understanding it to be some sort of a metaphysical intrusion. It is difficult to ignore the scriptural parallel from Acts 2:2, "And suddenly there came from heaven a sound like a mighty rushing wind" portending the arrival of the Holy Spirit at Pentecost for the Apostles.[15] The discussion continued back in Lewis's room, with the topic shifting to Christianity. Tolkien tapped out at 3 a.m., but Lewis and Dyson continued talking for another hour before getting into bed at 4 a.m.

In the subsequent letter to Arthur, dated just eight days later, Lewis informs Arthur that "I have just passed on from believing in God to definitely believing in Christ – in Christianity. I will try to explain this another time. My long night talk with Dyson and Tolkien had a good deal to do with it."[16] This admission marks the linear end point of Lewis's progression from atheist—recalling Lewis's early letters to Arthur writing, "I believe in no religion"—to deist—"In the Trinity Term of 1929 I gave in, and admitted god was God, and knelt and prayed: perhaps, that night, the most dejected and reluctant convert in all England"[17]—to now professing Christian.

In the final letter in the trilogy to Arthur about his evening at Addison's Walk, Lewis explicates in more depth the significance of his evening with Tolkien and Dyson. It seems the final barrier for Lewis that prohibited his full acceptance of Christianity was the concept of redemption. Lewis acknowledges that there may be a need for redemption from eternal separation from God as a result of sin, but he tells Arthur that the real struggle has been with "how the life and death of Someone Else (whoever he was) 2000 years ago could help us here and now – except in so far as his example

---

14. Lewis, *Collected Letters*, 1:970
15. Acts 2:2.
16. Lewis, *Collected Letters*, 1:974.
17. Lewis, *Surprised by Joy*, 228.

helped us."[18] Christ's death on the cross as the atonement for sinful humanity had seemed to him either "silly or shocking."[19] It was just here that Tolkien and Dyson rendered their most important service to Lewis by making him see that the idea of sacrifice in pagan stories and the accompanying meaning and significance behind those stories were palatable to Lewis, yet sacrifice within the Christian story with its accompanying meaning and significance was not. If Lewis had accepted the one, he could now accept the other, writing Arthur, "Now the story of Christ is simply a true myth: a myth working on us in the same way as the others, but with this tremendous difference that it really happened."[20] Lewis's recognition of Christ's death and resurrection as a factual event within the course of human history meant he was free to treat it as he had treated other stories and myths, with the important distinction that among all myths "it is the most important and full of meaning."[21]

There is no generic template for a conversion to Christianity. Lewis records in *Surprised by Joy* that on a date somewhere between Lewis's first letter to Arthur regarding his night on Addison's Walk, September 20, 1931, and the last letter, dated October 18, 1931, he was riding in the sidecar of Warnie's motorcycle, and that "When we set out I did not believe that Jesus Christ is the Son of God, and when I reached the zoo I did."[22] The gospel message resonates differently in the heart of each believer preceding one's surrendering their life to following Christ. Conversion may occur over a short period of time, while for some it may take a lifetime. The time of Lewis's conversion really began with his series of three "Dry Tree" letters to Arthur about beauty while convalescing from his war injuries as he realized that there was something or Someone outside his closed materialist universe. At the final decision point regarding Christianity in the sidecar on the way to the zoo,

18. Lewis, *Collected Letters*, 1:976.

19. Lewis, *Collected Letters*, 1:976.

20. Lewis, *Collected Letters*, 1:977.

21. Lewis, *Collected Letters*, 1:977.

22. Lewis, *Surprised by Joy*, 237.

his intellectual assent was the next logical progression in his reasoning process. However, Lewis's conversion took more than mere intellectual assent. Lewis had found meaning in Christianity in that it had fulfilled his unsatisfied desire and longing, or Joy.

Lewis's conversion to Christianity had caused an ideological shift in his intellectual framework, and perhaps the best way for him to crystallize what had happened to him was to write it down. He did this over a two-week period while spending his summer holiday at Arthur's home in Ireland from August 15 through August 29, 1932.[23] Most go on summer vacation to relax. Lewis went on summer vacation to write, and the result was the allegorical *The Pilgrim's Regress*, reflecting Lewis's own faith journey and similar in structure to John Bunyan's *The Pilgrim's Progress*. In Lewis's story, the main character, John, envisions an island governed by a "Landlord." The vision of this island arouses in him "a sweetness and a pang"[24] that connects back to Lewis's description of "the memory of a memory" or the "longing of a longing" in *Surprised by Joy*. The remainder of the story consists of John's journey to find the island, where along the way he meets different characters who either help or impede him on his journey, such as Mr. Enlightenment, Mr. Sensible, or Mother Kirk, who represents "Traditional Christianity."[25] All these characters serve to represent narratives found in Lewis's own path to Christianity.

Aside from the story itself, what might be most astonishing about *The Pilgrim's Regress* is the quickness with which it was written. In the editor's introduction to the Wade Center's annotated edition of *The Pilgrim's Regress*, David Downing comments, "It may also be the first book composed in two weeks that is still in print eight decades later!"[26] Lewis's letter to Arthur on August 11 confirming his arrival on the August 15 doesn't portend the creative outburst that would accompany his visit: "I am so tired that our old roles will be reversed: you will be the one who wants to

23. Lewis, *Collected Letters*, 2:86.
24. Lewis, *Pilgrim's Regress*, 12.
25. Lewis, *Pilgrim's Regress*, 73.
26. Lewis, *Pilgrim's Regress*, xvii.

walk further and sit up later and talk more."[27] It would have been fascinating to be a fly on the wall and listen to the back-and-forth between Lewis and Arthur during Lewis's creative process as he reconstructed his intellectual and spiritual journey. Lewis gives us a peak into one of these exchanges in a letter from later that year responding to Arthur's criticism that *The Pilgrim's Regress* may be too complex. Lewis reminds Arthur about a conversation during their time together from the summer when they were discussing the meaning of Christ's statement, "Truly, I say to you, unless you turn and become like children, you will never enter the kingdom of heaven."[28] Arthur seems to have interpreted Christ's words to mean that those beginning their faith journeys must accept the tenets of Christianity like a child unquestioningly following the directive of a parent, while Lewis felt that the motive behind accepting that directive must be pure.

Arthur's role in the writing of *The Pilgrim's Regress* constituted more than just a host and sounding board. He played a role in the editorial process too. In December of 1932, Lewis sent him the manuscript with the request that Arthur assist him with suggestions on the "style" of the work. Just before publication, Lewis confirms to Arthur, "I did adopt many of your corrections, or at least made alterations where you objected. So if the book is a ghastly failure I shall always say 'Ah it's this Arthur business.'"[29]

There were many friends who played important roles in helping C. S. Lewis along his journey to faith, and Lewis names and recognizes them in *Surprised by Joy* and other places. But it was Arthur Greeves who was the faithful witness from the first step to the last, both the literal journey that culminated in the sidecar of Warnie's motorcycle on the way to the zoo and the allegorical journey chronicled in *The Pilgrim's Regress*. Lewis recognized this as well. In telling Arthur he was dedicating *The Pilgrim's Regress* to him, Lewis writes, "It is yours by every right – written in your house, read to you as it was written, and celebrating (at least in the

27. Lewis, *Collected Letters*, 2:86.

28. Matthew 18:3. This story is also found in Mark 10:15 and Luke 18:17.

29. Lewis, *Collected Letters*, 2:104.

most important parts) an experience which I have more in common with you than anyone else."[30]

30. Lewis, *Collected Letters*, 2:104.

CHAPTER 6

"Homeliness"

LONG BEFORE C. S. Lewis's ride in the sidecar of his brother Warnie's motorcycle where he finally determined that Jesus Christ is
the Son of God, Lewis had been wrestling with other issues along
his pilgrimage to Christianity. He had confided in Arthur on such
topics as temptation, anger, doubt, chastity, and pride, joining millions of other pilgrims who along their own journeys to faith in
Christ have wrestled with the same things.

One issue Lewis expresses struggling with particularly in
these preconversion letters is pride, which he identifies as "my
besetting sin." A besetting sin is one that a person struggles with
continuously. They are referred to in Hebrews 12:1, where the
writer exhorts us to "lay aside every weight, and the sin which
doth so easily beset us, and let us run with patience the race that
is set before us."[1] In a January 1930 letter to Arthur, Lewis finds
that, to his shock and disappointment, in examining himself one
in every three of his thoughts "is a thought of self-admiration," and
that just when he manages to tamp down one of these thoughts
his pride wells up to congratulate himself on "What an admirable
fellow I am to have broken their necks!"[2] Lewis concludes this
letter by telling Arthur, "*Pride*, on the other hand, is the mother of

1. Hebrews 12:1 (KJV).
2. Lewis, *Collected Letters*, 1:878.

all sins."[3] Lewis's conviction that pride is the worst of all sins was a belief he would hold to his whole life. In *Mere Christianity*, Lewis devotes a whole chapter, titled "The Great Sin," to pride, asserting that it "leads to every other sin: it is the complete anti-God state of mind."[4]

During this period of self-reflection prior to his conversion, Lewis measured himself against the Christian idea of chastity. Whether chastity for Lewis meant physical chastity or mental chastity it is impossible to say, especially without speculating on the nature of his relationship with Janie Moore. The facts as we are aware of them include the reality that just prior to his conversion to Christianity he and Janie Moore had shared the same residence for ten years and would continue to do so for the remainder of her life. Lewis was also aware that one of the central tenets of Christian teaching is that sexual relations are reserved for husbands and wives within the bond of matrimony. Absent specificity, all we know is that in early 1930 Lewis tells Arthur "that I seem to have been supported in respect to chastity and anger more continuously, and with less struggle, for the last ten days or so than I often remember to have been."[5]

Like the rest of us, specific vices for Lewis did not remain unaccompanied; they bled into each other. Anger is another issue Lewis wrote Arthur about, and when mentioned it is coupled with pride. In describing how good anger can feel, Lewis writes that its "pleasure" is sourced, "I believe, in the fact that one feels entirely righteous oneself only when one is angry."[6] There is a prideful sense of superiority in an angry person that makes one feel better about oneself. Pride involves cutting others down in order to raise yourself up, and the combination of pride and anger can be found in Lewis's heartfelt and transparent admission to Arthur, "You have no idea how much of my time I spend just hating people whom

---

3. Lewis, *Collected Letters*, 1:878.

4. Lewis, *Mere Christianity*, 122.

5. Lewis, *Collected Letters*, 1:877.

6. Lewis, *Collected Letters*, 1:950.

I disagree with – tho' I know them only from their books – and inventing conversations in which I score off them."[7]

There is a marked undulation in Lewis's preconversion letters characterized by wide swings in his spiritual self-diagnosis. At times, Lewis exhibits optimism regarding his condition, such as when he tells Arthur, "Things are going very well for me (spiritually)." Conversely, in a remarkable letter dated Christmas Eve 1930, a date on which for many the mood is festive, Lewis is contemplative, finding himself at the other end of spectrum, writing, "One falls so often that it hardly seems worth while picking oneself up and going through the farce of starting over as if you could ever hope to walk."[8] Lewis was experiencing the natural ebb and flow of the spiritual life that everyone experiences as they work out their faith with fear and trembling.[9] This sense of despair Lewis is suffering from is his own fault and he tells Arthur that it comes from his "old sceptical habits, and the spirit of the age, and the cares of the day," leaving him with the feeling that when he prays, "I wonder if I am not posting letters to a non-existent address."[10] Every Christian has stood in solidarity with Lewis on the matter of doubt. Doubt is actually a sign of a healthy faith. Mindless belief is constructed on a weak foundation and will crumble when life's difficulties arise, but a faith that's been sincerely examined and thought out will remain when the harshness of life does its worst.

If there is one letter in the 276 letters to Arthur Greeves spanning their nearly fifty-year friendship that is most representative of their relationship, it is found among these preconversion letters as Lewis continued his deep dive into self-reflection of his various sins and behaviors. It is a four-page letter dated April 30, 1930, yet much of the letter no longer exists because Arthur destroyed most of it. What remains reveals the very stratum of the friendship between C. S. Lewis and Arthur Greeves. The letter begins with an apology from Lewis to Arthur for not writing sooner, followed

7. Lewis, *Collected Letters*, 2:125–26.

8. Lewis, *Collected Letters*, 1:945.

9. Philippians 2:12.

10. Lewis, *Collected Letters*, 1:944.

by details of an upcoming walking tour with Owen Barfield and others. Lewis then reports that Janie Moore had invited Warnie to reside with them at the Kilns, followed by Lewis's concern for Warnie making the transition to domestic life.

The letter must have taken a very dramatic turn because Walter Hooper informs us that Arthur had written in pencil at the top of the first page, "very private" and "to be burnt." What remains of the letter is the fourth page, which begins, "have fallen so far below – MYSELF!!! Which is rather like a man repenting for being drunk because it was unworthy of his career as a forger."[11] The letter continues, "I hadn't meant to give you such a dose of myself – but there is hardly any of it that I can say to any one but you and it is a relief to let it out."[12]

No one will ever know what secrets C. S. Lewis told Arthur Greeves that required their destruction. Was it Lewis who asked Arthur to destroy these revelations, or did Arthur, realizing their extremely sensitive nature, take it upon himself to destroy them? We will never know. But this letter does show that Lewis was aware of his true spiritual state. When he uses the simile comparing himself to a drunk repenting for reflecting negatively on his career as a forger, Lewis shows he clearly understood that he was a "forger," and that he stood in solidarity with the rest of humanity in a sinful condition. This letter also shows that Lewis understood the importance of confession, a spiritual practice he would more formerly engage in with Fr. Walter Adams beginning around 1940.[13] Psalm 32:3 tells us, "For when I kept silent, my bones wasted away through my groaning all day long."[14] Whatever Lewis had told Arthur in this letter, at the end he feels a "relief" by getting it off his chest.

In the last line of this letter, we find the sentiment most representative of the friendship between C. S. Lewis and Arthur Greeves. Lewis concludes, "You are my only real Father Confessor

---

11. Lewis, *Collected Letters*, 1:888.
12. Lewis, *Collected Letters*, 1:888.
13. Lewis, *Collected Letters*, 2:1015.
14. Psalm 32:1.

so you owe me a line." Whatever it was that Lewis had done, whatever actions Lewis had committed that inspired one of them to destroy the evidence, it was to Arthur that Lewis went to unburden himself, and perhaps seek absolution. In this letter, Lewis unveils himself to Arthur with a transparency he showed no other person in his life.

While we don't know what events prompted the destruction of parts of this letter, readers who don't know that C. S. Lewis wasn't always a Christian may be shocked by some of the attitudes and behaviors early in his life. Each of us have said and done things we wish we had not. In our twenty-first-century world, almost everyone possesses a portable video recorder in their pocket in the form of a cell phone by which to record for all time words and actions we later wish we could take back. In Lewis's day, instead of TikTok videos or Facebook posts, letters were the medium that chronicled people's lives and sometimes altered them. Mary Queen of Scots and Marie Antoinette, among others, are examples of individuals who had unflattering information revealed after their letters were penned.

As C. S. Lewis was beginning to settle into his new Christianity, he had the opportunity to expunge his record of all the embarrassing events and thoughts he had chronicled to date in the 170 letters to Arthur spanning their then seventeen-year friendship. As part of Warnie's compilation of "The Memoirs of the Lewis Family," Lewis had written Arthur requesting that he return all the letters in his possession Lewis had written him so that they could be copied and included in the project. As Lewis reread the letters Arthur sent back, he was doing so from the vantage point of adulthood. As mentioned earlier, Lewis diagnosed his besetting sin as pride, and he recognized its tracks through the body of the letters, writing Arthur, "To me, as I re-read them, the most striking thing is their egoism: sometimes in the form of priggery, intellectual and even social: often in the form of downright affection (I seem to be posturing and showing off in every letter)."[15] Lewis did send back some letters he wanted to shield from Warnie that referred

15. Lewis, *Collected Letters*, 1:973.

to "It." While it cannot be said with certainty what "It" refers to in their early letters, the term obviously is used to allude to a code for something sexual, perhaps masturbation. Also sent back to Arthur were the letters that referred to Lewis's "pretended assignation with the Belgian girl," a confession that the proposed rendezvous was made up.

Once, when Lewis was just seventeen years old, he included this off-handed comment in one of his letters to Arthur: "I think you and I ought to publish our letters (they'd be a jolly interesting book by the way) under the title lamentations, as we are always jawing about our sorrows."[16] Looking back with hindsight many years later, Lewis doesn't really think doing so would be so "jolly." He finds, "How ironical that the very things wh. I was proud of in my letters then should make the reading of them a humiliation to me now!"[17]

The chain of custody of the early letters containing many of the unflattering thoughts, events, and behaviors of both C. S. Lewis and Arthur Greeves obviously begins with Arthur. After his death, they found their way to Lisbeth Greeves, the wife of Ronald Greeves, who was Arthur's first cousin. Lisbeth Greeves sent them to Warnie Lewis in late 1966. Walter Hooper happened to be visiting Warnie the day the letters arrived and Warnie charged Hooper with opening the package. Along with the batch of letters comprising the Lewis-Greeves correspondence was a note from Arthur's sister expressing Arthur's wish that the letters be sent to the Bodleian Library at Oxford University. Warnie completely disregarded these instructions and sent the letters to Wheaton College in Illinois. Later, in 1974, after Warnie had passed away, Lisbeth Greeves sent another batch of fifty letters written by C. S. Lewis to Arthur Greeves directly to Walter Hooper. These letters are from the period between 1949 through 1961.[18]

Why would Lewis turn down an opportunity to sanitize his history by destroying letters containing embarrassing elements?

16. Lewis, *Collected Letters*, 1:173.

17. Lewis, *Collected Letters*, 1:973.

18. Lewis, *They Stand Together*, 41.

The first reason was that Lewis understood that the letters were not his property, they belonged to Arthur. The recipient of a letter becomes the owner of the paper and ink used to compose the letter. To destroy or conveniently misplace some of these embarrassing letters would have constituted destroying Arthur's property. More importantly, as these letters contain "some of your secrets as well as mine,"[19] without these awkward revelations their friendship would not have had the depth and transparency that it did. The fact that each knew the other's secrets did not constitute one having dirt on the other. Rather, these shared revelations of the most personal nature served to knit the two closer together. Eventually, when the determination was made by the Lewis estate that all the known letters between C. S. Lewis and Arthur Greeves should be published, it was decided that there would be enough distance between the death of those involved and any potentially embarrassing public disclosures in their publication. As Walter Hooper described it when considering any revelations regarding Warnie Lewis's alcoholism, "there was now no 'face to be saved.'"[20]

The self-reflection in Lewis's preconversion letters continued postconversion, but in a different way. The Christian journey does not end at conversion. Saint Paul writes in 1 Thessalonians 4:3 that God's will for the follower of Christ is sanctification. Sanctification is the life-long process of being "transformed by the renewal of your mind,"[21] into the image of Christ. Sanctification was a part of the Christian journey Lewis took seriously, and we are eyewitnesses to Lewis's efforts at this undertaking in his postconversion letters to Arthur. The sanctification process involves making an honest assessment of the progress (or retreat) one is making regarding a specific sin over a period of time. As noted above, in letters to Arthur prior to Lewis's conversion, he confides to Arthur that pride is his besetting sin. Surrendering one's life to following Jesus doesn't make sin magically disappear; it merely makes one more aware of it. The letter noted previously where Lewis admitted

---

19. Lewis, *Collected Letters*, 1:973.

20. Lewis, *They Stand Together*, 41.

21. Romans 12:3.

to Arthur that he spent a good deal of time disliking people and inventing conversations in his mind to show how much smarter he was than them was written after his conversion.

Perhaps an indication of Lewis's progress regarding sanctification, specifically having to do with his besetting sin of pride, can be found in the introduction to the book *The Weight of Glory*, where Walter Hooper writes of his time with Lewis toward the end of Lewis's life. While discussing Sir Launcelot's comment about winning "worship" in Malory's *Morte d'Arthur*, Hooper reminded Lewis that he was "wining worship" with the popularity of his books.[22] Lewis responded to Hooper in a voice with the "most complete humility I've ever observed in anyone, 'One cannot be too careful *not* to think of it.'"[23]

Lewis's immediate postconversion letters to Arthur also reveal his developing theology. In a September 1933 letter, it appears Arthur had written Lewis and asked "how far God can sympathise with our evil will as well as with our good – or, to draw it milder, *whether* he does."[24] Lewis responds with a treatise expounding on the topics of evil and sin. One of the reasons why reading Lewis's letters are so interesting and enlightening, including letters not addressed to Arthur, is that he uses the technique of restating pertinent phrases from the sender's letter in his response. In laying the foundation for his answer to Arthur, Lewis restates Arthur's assertion that "God must have a potentiality of His opposite – evil"[25] and that there is "no good without evil."[26] Arthur's view of evil is a common one, consisting of the idea that there is a continuing struggle within the cosmos between two equal and opposite forces, good and evil, or God and Satan. The error in this view is that if God is the creator of all things, he must have then created evil. Fusing together two verses of Scripture, James 1:17 and John 1:5, Lewis reminds Arthur that God is the "Father of lights" and that

22. Lewis, *Weight of Glory*, 14.
23. Lewis, *Weight of Glory*, 14.
24. Lewis, *Collected Letters*, 2:121.
25. Lewis, *Collected Letters*, 2:121.
26. Lewis, *Collected Letters*, 2:122.

there is no darkness in him. As such, God could not have created anything evil.

Instead, Lewis turns the "no good without evil" statement on its head, telling Arthur that a more accurate assessment of evil is that there is "no evil without good."[27] This view of evil reflects the Augustinian view that evil is the privation of good.[28] At the end of the first chapter of Genesis, "God saw everything that he had made, and behold, it was very good."[29] Since God created nothing evil, evil is born only when sin begins to corrupt a person. Evil is like a leech that attaches itself and draws life from its host. Without a host, it will die. Lewis explains it to Arthur this way: "The truth is that evil is not a real thing at all, like God. It is simply good spoiled. That is why I say there can be good without evil, but no evil without good."[30]

As Lewis was undergoing the transformative process of developing and growing in his faith, he noticed a change in Arthur. It was not that Arthur had changed in his behavior toward Lewis. Instead, Lewis tells Arthur he feels "the centre of your interests might have shifted more than mine."[31] In one way, that may have been true, but it also may have been that Lewis began to view Arthur through the grid of his newfound Christian faith. One can begin to see the world and people differently with a Christian worldview. Lewis admits he has changed, but these changes are "natural developments of the original thing we had in common."[32]

Sensing these changes, Lewis began using a word in his letters to Arthur on a frequent basis as an incantation to pull Arthur back. The word Lewis uses is "homely." The "homely" for Lewis was a particular state of being or reality rooted in the beauty and ordinariness of the everyday. Examples of things that Lewis describes as homely in his letters to Arthur are certain books, like

---

27. Lewis, *Collected Letters*, 2:122.

28. Augustine, *Confessions*, 101.

29. Genesis 1:27.

30. Lewis, *Collected Letters*, 2:124.

31. Lewis, *Collected Letters*, 2:125.

32. Lewis, *Collected Letters*, 2:120.

Jeremy Taylor's *Rule and Exercise of Holy Living*[33] and Emily Bronte's *Wuthering Heights*,[34] and certain foods, such as "fried fish, ham and eggs, bread and cheese, and beer."[35] Lewis found certain places homely, such as Hillsboro, the home where he and Mrs. Moore primarily resided prior to moving to the Kilns.[36] He also had an eye for the homely, spying this invisible, yet to him obvious, quality while on a walk in a "pleasant mixture of ivies and low plants and mosses" that revealed "mysteries twining at our feet, where homeliness and magic embrace one another."[37]

If Arthur was changing as Lewis suggested, the use of the word "homely" provided Lewis with a means to remind Arthur of what still connected them. The frequency of the word's use suggests that he and Arthur shared a common understanding of its meaning and significance. In his tribute to Arthur in "The Memoirs of the Lewis Family," Lewis writes, "What he called the 'Homely' was the natural food both of his heart and his imagination. A bright hearth seen through an open door as we passed, a train of ducks following a brawny farmer's wife, a drill of cabbages in a suburban field – these were the things that never failed to move him even to an ecstasy."[38] Homeliness was both a state of being and a place. Lewis intended to use the word like a magnet to pull Arthur back from some of the changes he saw in him.

Unfortunately, Lewis's appeal to Arthur to remember the "Homely" does not appear to have worked. Quantitatively, the years 1930 and 1931 produced forty-seven letters from C. S. Lewis to Arthur. There is a significant decrease in the number of letters from Lewis for the rest of the decade. There were only two letters sent to Arthur in 1937, one in 1938, and one in 1939. For his part, Lewis tried to encourage a resumption of regular correspondence. In 1934, Lewis, Mrs. Moore, and Maureen Moore traveled through

33. Lewis, *Collected Letters*, 1:967.
34. Lewis, *Collected Letters*, 2:34.
35. Lewis, *Collected Letters*, 2:102.
36. Lewis, *Collected Letters*, 1:833.
37. Lewis, *Collected Letters*, 1:858.
38. Lewis, *They Stand Together*, 25.

Ireland and stopped to visit Arthur. After one six-month period between letters in 1935, Lewis writes, "I believe I could still make a fair attempt at regular correspondence, but you yourself vetoed that, and odd letters, like odd bills, I do find it hard to meet when I'm busy."[39]

Another cause of the infrequency of their letters could be that Lewis continued to collect new friends that developed into deep-rooted relationships during the 1930s. In a 1935 letter he tells Arthur that "friendship is the greatest of all worldly goods. Certainly to me it is the chief happiness of life."[40] In fact, friendship for Lewis was so important that if he could give a piece of advice to a young person trying to decide where to live, he would tell them to "sacrifice almost everything to live where you can be near your friends."[41] In addition to his friendships with Tolkien, Barfield, and Dyson, Lewis added a former student, Alan Griffiths, later more commonly known as the Catholic monk Dom Bede Griffiths. Lewis describes Griffiths to Arthur as "a magnificent looking creature – a dark Celt, but very big."[42] Lewis served as Griffiths's tutor and at the time neither was a Christian. The arc of their spiritual trajectory was similar in that both converted to Christianity in 1931.

Griffiths was living as a minimalist with two other men in a cottage on the outskirts of Oxford when he began reading the Bible. He was received into the Catholic Church on Christmas Eve 1931. Just as Owen Barfield had attempted to engage Lewis in discussions about Anthroposophy, Griffiths sought to engage Lewis in discussions regarding Catholicism. And just as he had done with Barfield, Lewis closed the door, writing, "And while I am on the subject, I had better say once and for all that I do not intend to discuss with you in the future, if I can help it, any of the questions at issue between our respective churches."[43] Though

39. Lewis, *Collected Letters*, 2:169.
40. Lewis, *Collected Letters*, 2:174.
41. Lewis, *Collected Letters*, 2:174.
42. Lewis, *Collected Letters*, 1:881.
43. Lewis, *Collected Letters*, 2:135.

Lewis didn't want to discuss the differences between Anglicanism and Catholicism with Griffiths, Lewis did lean on him for help in constructing the BBC talks that would eventually turn into the book *Mere Christianity*, and, as he had done with his other close friends, Lewis paid tribute to Griffiths by dedicating *Surprised by Joy* to him.

Still another important friendship for Lewis that blossomed out of this period in his life was with Charles Williams. Book reviews and recommendations were an integral part the correspondence between C. S. Lewis and Arthur Greeves, and in a February 26, 1936, letter toArthur, Lewis excitedly tells him, "I have just read what I think is a really great book."[44] The book was Williams's "Christian fantasy" novel *The Place of the Lion*. The book had such an effect on Lewis that he soon composed a fan letter to Williams. In his gushing tribute, he tells Williams that "it is to me one of the major literary events of my life."[45] Lewis tells Williams about an "informal club called the Inklings"[46] that he belongs to where the only requirements for inclusion "are a tendency to write, and Christianity."[47] He invites Williams up to Oxford to spend the night and attend an Inklings gathering.

Williams was employed by Oxford University Press in their London office as a proofreader. Providentially, as Lewis was penning his note to Williams, Williams was reviewing Lewis's book *The Allegory of Love*. The very next day Williams responded in kind to Lewis's letter, telling him that not since Dante had he come across a book "that shows the slightest understanding of what this very peculiar identity of love and religion means."[48] This mutual admiration quickly took root, with Lewis remembering "our friendship grew inward to the bone," and when the London office of Oxford University Press had to be moved to Oxford in 1939 because of World War II, Williams was able to begin attending the

44. Lewis, *Collected Letters*, 2:180.
45. Lewis, *Collected Letters*, 2:183.
46. Lewis, *Collected Letters*, 2:183.
47. Lewis, *Collected Letters*, 2:183.
48. Lewis, *Collected Letters*, 2:184.

Inklings meetings and he and Lewis were able to see much more of each other.

By the time Charles Williams made his first appearance at an Inklings gathering, the group had congealed to self-generate a radiant energy of didactic conversation, English masculinity, and jovial banter. Lewis provides a succinct description of their activities: "We smoked, talked, argued, and drank together."[49] They did far more than that. The Inklings was birthed out of Tolkien's informal group the Kolbitars, and the name Inklings was coopted from a defunct literary club that Tolkien and Lewis had previously attended. Generally, the Inklings met twice weekly. They gathered Tuesdays at the now renowned Eagle and Child, a public house located on St. Giles Street in Oxford, and then congregated at Lewis's rooms at Magdalen on Thursday nights. The Thursday-evening meetings were centered around one of the attendees reading out loud something they were currently writing. While never a formal club, a non-exclusive list of regular attenders includes Tolkien, Barfield, Dyson, Coghill, Warnie, Lord David Cecil, and Lewis's physician, Robert Havard. Writing in *The Four Loves*, Lewis observes, "Friendship (as the ancients saw) can be a school of virtue; but also (as they did not see) a school of vice . . . It makes good men better and bad men worse."[50] The Inklings certainly made Lewis, already a good man, better, in that it satiated his deep-seated need for male friendship and camaraderie.

Many of us have wondered what it would have been like to sit in on an Inklings meeting. While every member of the Inklings was tremendously accomplished, perhaps the most relatable to the rest of us was Lewis's physician, Dr. Robert Havard, in that he was neither a professor nor a writer. This is not to imply that the Inklings was exclusively a group of literary academicians. Barfield was a lawyer and Warnie was a soldier. Dr. Havard first met C. S. Lewis while making a house call to the Kilns when Lewis was sick with the flu. He diagnosed Lewis in five minutes and then the two spent the next thirty minutes talking philosophy. Havard

49. Lewis, *Essays*, v.
50. Lewis, *Four Loves*, 80.

described the typical Inklings meeting as too many people speaking at once and the reader who was in the dock before the group complaining that he couldn't get a word in edgewise.[51] One example of the jocularity that permeated the group was the accumulation of nicknames pinned on Havard. He was alternately referred to as "Humphrey," "the U.Q." (short for Useless Quack), and "The Red Admiral," after he returned from military sea duties with a ruddy-colored beard.[52] In reality, this teasing was a sign of respect and admiration. Lewis thought highly enough of Havard to ask him to contribute an appendix at the conclusion of *The Problem of Pain* on the physical effects of pain. In *The Problem of Pain* he also continued his tradition of dedicating books to his friends, this time "To The Inklings."

Even though the letters between Lewis and Greeves became less frequent after Lewis's conversion to Christianity, the foundation their friendship was constructed on remained solid. In a March 1933 letter, Lewis laments the decline in the frequency of their correspondence, writing, "Fortunately each feels sure that the cause of this decline, whatever else it may be, is no diminution of the friendship."[53] All the qualities that mark their deep friendship are still there. At one point in early 1930, Arthur must have had a book proposal rejected and Lewis penned a lengthy response of encouragement drawing on his own failures and experiences as a writer. Lewis's bibliography up to that point consisted of the books *Spirits in Bondage*, a collection of his poems published in 1919, and *Dymer*, a long narrative poem published in 1926. In his response Lewis tells Arthur that he can empathize with how he is feeling. Lewis even includes a copy of a rejection letter he received when he submitted *Dymer* for publication. Not only does Lewis provide empathy, but he also goes beyond by issuing Arthur warnings about the writing life and life in general based on his own experiences as a writer. He tells Arthur, "From the age of sixteen onwards I had one single ambition, from which I never wavered,

51. Como, ed., *C. S. Lewis at the Breakfast Table*, 217.
52. Como, ed., *C. S. Lewis at the Breakfast Table*, 222.
53. Lewis, *Collected Letters*, 2:101.

in the prosecution of which I spent every ounce I could, on wh. I really & deliberately staked my whole contentment."[54] Lewis has had a book published and, instead of finding the fulfillment he thought he would, he has found only the feeling of failure. Seeking fulfillment as a writer, he tells Arthur, is an "*absolute delusion*."[55]

Lewis reminds Arthur that he is praying for him: "By the way, when you ask me to 'pray for you' . . . I don't know if you are serious, but the answer is, I do."[56] Prayer had a dual purpose for Lewis. The first is petitionary. We bring our requests regarding the other person before God. The second involves the person doing the praying. Prayer has an effect on the person doing the praying. Lewis tells Arthur that his prayers may not do Arthur any good, "but it does me a lot, for I cannot ask for any change to be made in you without finding that the very same needs to be made in me; which pulls me up and also by putting us all in the same boat checks any tendency to priggishness."[57] This idea about prayer working on the person offering the prayer is one Lewis would retain his entire life. In his book *Letters to Malcom*, written six months before his death, Lewis makes a similar point in that when we earnestly pray and unveil ourselves before God with a desire will to be known by Him, "The change is in us."[58]

54. Lewis, *Collected Letters*, 1:925.

55. Lewis, *Collected Letters*, 1:925.

56. Lewis, *Collected Letters*, 2:53.

57. Lewis, *Collected Letters*, 2:53.

58. Lewis, *Collected Letters to Malcolm*, 21.

CHAPTER 7

"A New Gap"

ON SEPTEMBER 3, 1939, Britain declared war against Germany. A few days earlier, Germany had invaded Poland. Like a line of dominos toppling, Britain was joined by France and Australia in declaring war against Germany, and soon almost all of Europe was engulfed in the Second World War. Having lived through the First World War, Lewis new exactly what this meant. Writing just after Britain's declaration of war, he tells Arthur, "The next few years will be ghastly, but though my *nerves* are often staggered, my faith and reason are alright. I have no doubt that all this suffering will be for our ultimate good if we use it rightly . . . but I can't help wishing one could *hibernate* till it's all over."[1]

Lewis had served admirably in the First World War. Now there was a question of whether he would be required to actively serve again, and he was experiencing some apprehension about it. In conjunction with their declaration of war against Germany, the British Parliament enacted the National Service (Armed Forces) Act, which stipulated military conscription for all males between the ages of eighteen and forty-one. At the time, Lewis was forty years old and would not turn forty-one until a few months later on November 29. Fortunately, Lewis was not called to active service, but he did have a small role, patrolling Oxford one night out of

1. Lewis, *Collected Letters*, 2:274.

every nine with the Home Guard. He writes to Arthur that this consists of "mouching about the most depressing and malodorous parts of Oxford with a rifle."[2]

While Lewis is prescient in his predictions to Arthur about the coming war, as it was "ghastly," he concludes his letter with an interesting personal observation about how the war will impact him specifically. For Lewis, "the war has come in the nick of time: I was just beginning to get too well settled in my profession, too successful, and probably self complacent."[3] For most, the prospect of a looming war would be met with fear and anxiety. Will I live through the war? Will my family? Will my home be destroyed? How will the rhythms of my daily life be disrupted? Instead, Lewis tells Arthur that he is in one sense welcoming it as a self-corrective. The coming hardships would recenter him, maybe even spiritually, as his success and profession have become too important.

The war also affected Arthur. By 1941, the air attacks from the German Luftwaffe eventually intensified across Great Britain, extending all the way to Belfast. On April 16, Belfast sustained heavy damage from German bombs. Arthur was apparently serving as a warden, helping to oversee the civil air defense of Belfast. Word had reached Lewis via his childhood friend Jane McNeil that Arthur had exhibited bravery during the raid on Belfast. Lewis passed on McNeil's observation regarding Arthur's "courage and *decisiveness*" and then praised his friend by remarking, "Anyway, congratulations. The courage I always knew about – from many hair-raising occasions in your car."[4] During the war years, their correspondence slowed, with Lewis writing only about twice a year. This may have been the result of the conditions brought about by the war, but there may have been other factors involved as well. One factor was certainly that Lewis's circle of friends expanded out further (partly due to his growing fame as a writer and speaker). Still another was that Lewis was remarkably productive as a writer during this time. And a final factor for their slowing

2. Lewis, *They Stand Together*, 487.
3. Lewis, *Collected Letters*, vol 2, 274.
4. Lewis, *Collected Letters*, vol 2, 503.

correspondence was that he and Arthur were drifting apart theologically. Whether it was one of these factors or a combination of all of them, the result was that by the end of the 1940s Lewis feels "as if a new gap had opened between us."[5] Nonetheless, the lack of communication was not a reflection of any diminishing affection, as Lewis had told Arthur at the beginning of the war, "I never pass a day without remembering you."[6]

A further consequence of the war was that Oxford University Press moved some of their operations to Oxford, allowing Lewis to spend more time with his friend Charles Williams. Williams was just one of the many people Lewis would add to his growing circle of close friends during the 1940s. Thanks to Lewis, Williams seamlessly integrated himself into the Inkling's rhythms. Sadly, while Lewis's friendship with Williams deepened, it served as a wedge between Lewis and another other very close friend, J. R. R. Tolkien. In a letter to his son Michael shortly after Lewis died, Tolkien wrote, "We were separated first by the sudden apparition of Charles William, and then by his marriage."[7] After a few short years in Oxford, Williams died suddenly.

Williams's death caught Lewis and the Inklings by surprise. Just a few days after the Germans had surrendered to the Allied Forces in May of 1945, Williams was taken to the Radcliffe Infirmary for stomach pain. None of the other Inklings were aware of the seriousness of his condition. Lewis found out about Williams's death because he went Radcliffe Infirmary to visit Williams and drop off a book to him before going on to the Inkling's regularly scheduled Tuesday meeting.[8] Lewis assumed that he would be bringing the group some sort of message from Williams. Instead, he informed his friends that Williams had passed away.

It is obvious that Williams had some sort of gravitational pull on Lewis and that during his brief time in Oxford and with the Inklings Williams supplanted Arthur, Tolkien, and all others

---

5. Lewis, *Collected Letters*, vol 2, 908.

6. Lewis, *Collected Letters*, vol 2, 488.

7. Tolkien, *Collected Letters of J.R.R. Tolkien*, 341.

8. Lewis, *Essays*, xiv.

as the brightest light in the constellation of Lewis's friends. His death affected Lewis emotionally and spiritually. Emotionally, he grieved over Williams's death, calling it the greatest loss he had ever known.[9] This grief is expressed in a letter to his friend Mary Neylan: "I have also become much acquainted with grief now through the death of my great friend Charles Williams, my friend of friends, the comforter of all our little set, the most angelic."[10] Lewis elsewhere writes that "No event has so corroborated my faith in the next world as Williams did by simply dying."[11] While Williams would not be physically present to him, his memory would transcend the whole of this world and serve as a reminder that death never has the last word.

Though the Inklings were exclusively male, Lewis had a circle of close female friends. One of these friendships began just as the war was starting. An Anglican nun by the name of Sister Penelope Lawson read Lewis's recently published *Out of the Silent Planet* and, like thousands of others who read a Lewis book, wrote him a letter praising his work. As Lewis would do thousands of times after receiving a letter from a reader, he responded. It was a lengthy response, as Sister Penelope had included one of her own books, *God Persists: A Short Survey of World History in Light of Christian Faith*, in her letter to Lewis. Lewis thoroughly enjoyed the book, expounding on some of the book's themes. There was obviously something in Sister Penelope's thought that resonated with Lewis and their correspondence continued until Lewis's death.

Born Ruth Penelope Lawson, Sister Penelope took holy orders in 1912 at the age of twenty-two at the Convent of the Community of St. Mary the Virgin at Wantage, a town located near Oxford. Someone at the convent recognized the intellectual potential this young nun possessed and she was sent to Oxford to study theology. She was a gifted writer in her own right, publishing books on theology and translations of works of the early church fathers. Early in their friendship, Lewis sent her a manuscript of

9. Lewis, *Essays*, xiv.

10. Lewis, *Collected Letters*, 2:652.

11. Lewis, *Essays*, xiv.

The Screwtape Letters prior to its publication for safekeeping. He was concerned that his publisher's office might be destroyed in the bombings. "I enclose a MS of Screwtape. If it is not a trouble I shd. like you to keep it safe until the book is printed (in case the one the publisher has got blitzed) – after that it can be made into spills or used to stuff dolls or anything."[12]

The nature of their correspondence was remarkably personnel and revealing, in a similar manner to how Lewis revealed himself to Arthur. Just one month after entrusting *The Screwtape Letters* manuscript to her, Lewis writes, "I am writing, really, for company, for I am a sad Ass at the moment. I've been going through one of those periods when one can no longer disguise the fact that movement has been backward and not forward. All the sins one thought one had escaped have been back again as strong as ever."[13] Early in their friendship, Sister Penelope sent Lewis a picture of the Shroud of Turin, a piece of linen cloth purportedly bearing the facial image of Jesus Christ just before his crucifixion, and, indicative of his feelings for her, Lewis hung this picture on his bedroom wall, where it remained for the rest of his life.

Lewis and Sister Penelope were linked together on Sister Penelope's best-known work, a translation of Athanasius's *On the Incarnation*. At that time, nuns were not permitted to write or publish under their own name. Consequently, Sister Penelope's works are found under the name "A Member of CSMV" or "A Religious of CSMV." Lewis provided an introduction stressing the importance of reading old books. In turn, Sister Penelope dedicated the book to Lewis: "To/C.S.L./Witness and Teacher."[14]

Another of Lewis's close female friends was Dorothy Sayers. By the time they met in 1942, it was Sayers and not Lewis who was England's most recognizable public Christian. Lewis once remarked about her that "She was the first person of importance who ever wrote me a fan-letter."[15] Sayers had gained notoriety through

12. Lewis, *Collected Letters*, 2:493.
13. Lewis, *Collected Letters*, 2:495.
14. Lewis, *Collected Letters*, 2:603.
15. Lewis, *Collected Letters*, 3:p1400.

her popular Lord Peter Whimsey detective novels and then she emerged as a public theologian when the Church of England invited her to write a play to be performed in Canterbury Cathedral in 1936. She would be following in the footsteps of T. S. Eliot's *Murder in the Cathedral,* which was performed the year before.

Her play, *The Zeal of Thy House,* was extremely popular, serving as a pivot point in her work as a writer from primarily a detective novelist to playwright and Dante translator. This resulted in the BBC inviting her to write a play for their *Children's Hour* in 1939, followed by an invitation for what has turned out to be her most well-known body of work, the twelve plays that composed the drama *The Man Born to Be King,* which were aired beginning in December of 1941 and concluding in October 1942. The play was highly controversial in that Sayers told the gospel story using common everyday language. This upset those used to hearing the story of Jesus in more formalized and traditional vernacular. Both Sayers and Lewis were popularizers, Sayers by making the gospel story more accessible to those not used to hearing it and Lewis doing the same through the use of a lion named Aslan. *The Man Born to Be King* became an important tool for Lewis's own spiritual development throughout his life, once writing, "For my own part, I have re-read it every Holy Week since it first appeared and never re-read it without being deeply moved."[16]

Lewis's friendship with Sayers began when Sayers wrote Lewis and invited him to write a book for a series she envisioned to be called "Bridgeheads."[17] Though Lewis politely declined the offer, telling her that she should write the book herself, this invitation would be the beginning of a correspondence that would last until Sayers passed away unexpectedly in 1957. In one sense, it seems Lewis gravitated to Sayers for friendship for one of the same reasons he gravitated to Sister Penelope and his other close friends, in that there was an intellectual rigor that Lewis found invigorating. But in a different sense Lewis gravitated to Sayers for friendship because there was an edginess to her work and thought.

16. Lewis, *On Stories,* 93.
17. Lewis, *Collected Letters,* 2:1071.

Several years after her death, Lewis penned a letter to the literary magazine, *Encounter*, writing of Sayers, "I liked her, originally, because she liked me; later, for the extraordinary zest and edge to her conversation – as I like a high wind."[18] This "high wind" might have been generated by her sometimes-difficult life circumstances. After a series of failed romantic relationships, she found herself pregnant and unmarried, and placed her child to be raised by her cousin. Only a few people ever knew she was a mother—not even her parents, whom she was too ashamed to tell.

A third female friend of Lewis's was the poet Ruth Pitter. Prior to beginning their friendship, each was aware of the other. The two had a mutual friend in fellow Inkling Lord David Cecil. In 1942, Pitter read *The Screwtape Letters* and was taken in by them, telling Cecil, "I have found the book which has excited me more than anything has done for a long time – 'The Screwtape Letters.'"[19] She credited Lewis's BBC talks for her conversion to Christianity. At about the same time, Cecil shared some of Pitter's poetry with Lewis and Cecil informed her Lewis was "deeply struck & went off to buy your poems."[20] As with Sister Penelope and Dorothy Sayers, their friendship and correspondence began when Pitter wrote Lewis a letter and Lewis respond by inviting Pitter to meet.

Their correspondence centered around their mutual love of poetry and a mutual admiration of the other's works. Many have wondered why this relationship didn't flower into a romance as the two seemed perfectly suited for each other. Once, after visiting with Pitter in 1955, Lewis told his friend George Sayer that "if he were not a confirmed bachelor, Ruth Pitter would be the woman he would like to marry."[21] Sayer told Lewis that it wasn't too late. Lewis responded with, "Oh yes it is,' he said, 'I've burnt my boats.'"[22] What caused Lewis to burn his boats may have been his existing and complicated relationship with Joy Davidman

---

18. Lewis, *Collected Letters*, 3:1400.

19. Lewis, *Collected Letters*, 2:1061.

20. Lewis, *Collected Letters*, 2:1061.

21. Sayer, *Jack*, 348.

22. Sayer, *Jack*, 348.

Gresham, who by this time was living in the Headington area in Oxford. After Lewis's marriage to Joy in 1957, his relationship with Ruth Pitter cooled, as Pitter wrote, "I had been taught in my youth that a woman's friendship with a married man must be by the grace and favour of his wife, and as Joy recovered and lived on so amazingly, I did from time to time write to her: but there was never any reply."[23]

In addition to Lewis accumulating more friends who occupied his attention, another reason there were fewer letters between Lewis and Arthur during the war years was that Lewis was remarkably productive during this period. *Out of the Silent Planet*, the first in his space trilogy, was published in 1938. This was followed by his first apologetic work, *The Problem of Pain*, published in 1940. The work caught the eye of the BBC and they invited him to give a series of talks on the Christian faith. Lewis agreed, but first other ideas were percolating. One of these ideas came to him while sitting in church. Lewis thought a series of letters from one "elderly retired devil" to a younger devil about how to work on a "patient" would make for an "entertaining" book.[24] This idea was the inception of the book *The Screwtape Letters*. But before it came out in book form the letters began appearing in *The Guardian* beginning in May 1941. This was not *The Guardian* currently recognized as a major international news outlet, but instead a weekly Anglican publication.

The very next month, on June 8, Lewis climbed the steps to the canopied pulpit at the historic Church of St. Mary the Virgin at Oxford University and looked out upon one of the largest crowds ever assembled at the church to deliver his remarkable sermon "The Weight of Glory."[25] "According to Walter Hooper, it was a sermon "so magnificent" that it is "worthy of a place with some of the Church Fathers."[26] Against the backdrop of a country plunged into the death and carnage of World War II, Lewis expounds on

---

23. Lewis, *Collected Letters*, 2:1064.
24. Lewis, *Collected Letters*, 2:426.
25. Lewis, *Weight of Glory*, 17.
26. Lewis, *Weight of Glory*, 17.

the themes of desire and glory. In eternity, Lewis points out, our connection to glory will be sourced in "the divine accolade, 'Well done, thou good and faithful servant.'" Thinking about our own eternal glory does not excuse us from thinking about our neighbor's glory. Instead, Lewis notes that "The load, or weight, or burden of my neighbor's glory should be laid on my back." This reality should change how we look at our neighbors because they are "the holiest object presented to your senses."[27]

In August, Lewis delivered his first set of talks for the BBC in four fifteen-minute increments on "Right and Wrong: A Clue to Meaning in the Universe."[28] A few months later, Lewis gave a series of lectures on Milton at University College, North Wales, in December. These lectures were published in 1942 into the book *A Preface to Paradise Lost*, dedicated to Charles Williams.[29] The very next month, in January of 1942, he began a series of five talks for the BBC, "What Christians Believe." These were followed by eight more BBC talks on "Christian Behavior" from September through November. In 1943, he published the second book in his space trilogy, *Perelandra*, wrote the third book in the series, *That Hideous Strength*, and gave a series of lectures at the University of Durham that would become *The Abolition of Man*. In early 1944, he gave the last of his talks for the BBC, seven talks entitled "Beyond Personality."

The resulting notoriety from all Lewis's activity, particularly his BBC talks, produced one undesirable effect. He began to receive a steady stream of letters from listeners and readers that would continue for the rest of his life. After the first series of broadcast talks in 1941, Lewis writes Arthur, "I had an enormous pile of letters from strangers to answer. One gets funny letters after broadcasting – some from lunatics who sign themselves 'Jehovah' or begin 'Dear Mr. Lewis, I was married at age 20 to a man I didn't love' – but many from serious inquirers whom it was my duty to

27. Lewis, *Weight of Glory*, 46.
28. Hooper, *C. S. Lewis*, 28.
29. Hooper, *C. S. Lewis*, 35.

answer fully."[30] The daily letter-writing would be a continuous thorn in Lewis's side and would become a part of his daily routine, telling Arthur that it composes "an hour and a half or two hours every morning before I can get to my own work."[31] Letter-writing took up valuable time during the day that could have been used for Lewis's other writing. Yet he believed that answering these letters was a part of his calling, especially due to the nature of the content of some of the letters. He once wrote Arthur, "my correspondence involves a great number of theological letters already which can't be neglected because they are answers to people in great need of help & often in great misery."[32]

The flurry of activity and productivity by Lewis during this period is stunning considering Lewis had his regular teaching obligations, he was housing evacuated girls from London at the Kilns, he was participating in middle-of-the-night Home Guard patrols, and he was providing increasing care for Mrs. Moore (Janie Moore had suffered a stroke in 1944). Lewis had learned the secret of being able to operate among the chaos. In a letter to Arthur composed just before Christmas, 1943, he notes, "Things are pretty bad here."[33] Mrs. Moore had a varicose ulcer that was getting worse, he was having trouble finding domestic help, and emotionally, "Sometimes I am very unhappy."[34] Yet, as difficult as all these distractions seemed to be, Lewis had come to the realization that they were a part of God's providence, telling Arthur, "The truth is of course that what one calls the interruptions are precisely one's real life – the life God is sending one day by day: what one calls one's 'real life' is a phantom of one's own imagination."[35] Many believe that our real lives should consist of continuous uninterrupted happiness, but Lewis was able to grasp that our real lives are lived through the stream of daily interruptions, through

30. Lewis, *Collected Letters*, 2:504.
31. Lewis, *Collected Letters*, 2:789.
32. Lewis, *Collected Letters*, 3:109.
33. Lewis, *Collected Letters*, 2:595.
34. Lewis, *Collected Letters*, 2:595.
35. Lewis, *Collected Letters*, 2:595.

illness, through anxiety, and through sadness. How else could he have been so productive during this period?

A final factor in the diminution of letters during this period between Lewis and Arthur was that there was an obvious widening of the gap theologically between the two. There are hints in earlier letters that Arthur may have been questioning some of the creedal beliefs of orthodox Christianity as a result of listening to other voices. In a letter from December 1931, Lewis addresses an assertion made by Arthur's cousin, Sir Frederick Lucius O'Brien, regarding the doctrine of the atonement not being found in the Gospels.[36] Christ's death is a historical event reported by the authors of the four Gospels. What his death means and its significance is explicated in the remainder of the New Testament by its writers. Whether Christ died as a ransom ("who gave himself as a ransom for all"[37]), or a propitiation ("He is the propitiation for our sins"[38]), or as our reconciliation to God ("we were reconciled to God by the death of his Son"[39]) has been the subject of theological debate. O'Brien's argument, as restated by Lewis, was "that the evangelists would have put the doctrine of atonement into the Gospel if they had had the slightest excuse, and, since they didn't, therefore Our Lord didn't teach it."[40]

Lewis's view of the doctrine of the atonement is a somewhat controversial one. This stems from his remarks in *Mere Christianity* where he seems to insinuate that if the idea of Christ dying as a punishment for our sins serves as an obstacle to accepting Christianity, one may simply disregard the idea.[41] In fact, he admits that the idea once seemed "silly" to him.[42]

Taken as a standalone, Lewis's remarks on the atonement in *Mere Christianity* could seem disconcerting. But before

36. Lewis, *Collected Letters*, 3:22.

37. 2 Timothy 2:6.

38. 1 John 2:2.

39. Romans 5:10.

40. Lewis, *Collected Letters*, 2:35.

41. Lewis, *Mere Christianity*, 55.

42. Lewis, *Mere Christianity*, 54.

pronouncing any final judgment on his view of the doctrine of the atonement, one must balance that consideration out with the fact that perhaps the apex of all Lewis's writing takes place on a stone tablet in Narnia, where the great lion Aslan reminds us of a deeper magic, "that when a willing victim who had committed no treachery was killed in a traitor's stead, the Table would crack and Death itself would start working backwards."[43]

Lewis's answer to Arthur regarding O'Brien's claim that the doctrine of the atonement is not present in the Gospel centers on the apostles' direct link to Christ, in that "we know from the Epistles that the Apostles (who had actually known him) did teach this doctrine in his name immediately after his death, it is clear that he did teach it:"[44] His answer also includes a not-so-subtle dig at Arthur's family members, as Lewis points out that they "have been found very ill grounded in the Bible itself and as ignorant as savages of the historical and theological reading needed to make the Bible more than superstition."[45]

The names of Arthur's other family members pop up again concerning theological differences with Lewis. Arthur's cousin, Lisbeth Greeves, is mentioned in a series of letters to Arthur beginning in 1944, each containing points where Arthur and Lewis seem to diverge theologically. Walter Hooper writes that Lisbeth Greeves described herself as "rebel against some of the beliefs of the Church, and in 1955 she became a member of the Baha'i Faith."[46] Arthur must have written to Lewis telling him of Lisbeth's beliefs about heaven and how they didn't align with Lewis's, yet Lewis didn't seem to want to fully engage, diffusing the situation.[47] It appears that Lisbeth Greeves also attempted to communicate with Lewis regarding theological matters because in a letter from 1952

43. C. S. Lewis, *Lion, Witch, Wardrobe*, 163.

44. Lewis, *Collected Letters*, 2:35.

45. Lewis, *Collected Letters*, 2:23.

46. Lewis, *They Stand Together*, 501.

47. Lewis, *They Stand Together*, 501.

Lewis tells Arthur to thank her for him, but "She will understand, I am sure, why I don't want to continue the discussion by post."[48]

The very next letter to Arthur reflects the widening theological gap between the two, with Lewis calling Arthur's view of the divinity of Christ "an old bone of contention between us."[49] The divinity of Christ has been an established doctrine of the Christian faith since the First Ecumenical Council at Nicea in 325 A.D. When millions of worshipers around the world recite the Nicene Creed each Sunday, they proclaim that Jesus Christ is "God from God, Light from Light, true God from true God." If Jesus isn't divine, then the Christian concept of the Trinity dissolves as well. This seems to be the point Lewis makes in his lengthy answer to Arthur. In addition to reminding Arthur that Arianism, an early movement withing the history of the church that taught Jesus is less than his Father, had been soundly discredited by the fifth century, Lewis writes that Christ's divinity is "not something stuck on which you can't unstick but something that peeps out at every point so that you'd have to unravel the whole web to get rid of it."[50] For Lewis, an honest reading of the four Gospels does not ask where Jesus makes his claims to divinity, but where does he not. Jesus's claim to divinity is a thread that runs through each of them.

What is interesting about this letter is that it is dated December 1944. Lewis had recently concluded delivering the last of his series of talks on Christianity that would eventually be published as *Mere Christianity*. The substance of the talks included the divinity of Christ. One might assume that as Lewis's good friend Arthur would have listened to these broadcasts. After hearing his friend Lewis expound on who Jesus was and is on national radio, and after receiving a thoughtful reply on the same topic, Walter Hooper reports that, sadly, Arthur wrote across the letter, "Not a good argument."[51]

---

48. Lewis, *Collected Letters*, 3:103.
49. Lewis, *Collected Letters*, 3:502.
50. Lewis, *They Stand Together*, 503.
51. Lewis, *They Stand Together*, 502.

Other topics Arthur appears to have asked or challenged Lewis on in the next few letters include hell and what Arthur suggested was Lewis's "emphasis on material things."[52] We cannot say with certainty what Arthur's specific objections were regarding material things, but we can, from Lewis's remarks, find ourselves in the general vicinity. As an Anglican, the use of the phrase "material things" by Lewis and presumably by Arthur point toward sacramentalism. Generally, a sacrament such as Communion or baptism is viewed as an outward and visible sign of an inward and spiritual grace. Using the material elements of bread, water, and wine, and sanctifying them by Word and Spirit, the transcendent spiritual reality of Christ and his grace is manifested though the created order. Lewis had been a regular communicant after his conversion to Christianity, beginning with his first meaningful Communion on Christmas Day 1931.

As with Arthur's objections to what he believed was Lewis's focus on material things, there was obviously discussion between the two regarding the idea of hell, because Lewis felt it was necessary to clarify his views about it to Arthur. The concept of hell was a backdrop to Lewis's books *The Screwtape Letters*, *A Preface to Paradise Lost*, and *The Great Divorce*. Lewis did not intend for these fictional works to be theological pronouncements. Instead, writing in an early preface to *The Screwtape Letters*, his intention "was not to speculate about diabolical life but to throw light from a new angle on the life of men."[53] This letter to Arthur tells us more regarding Lewis's thoughts on the infernal: "About Hell. All I have ever said is that the N.T. plainly implies the possibility of some being finally left in 'the outer darkness.'"[54] The mention of "outer darkness" is an allusion to several verses in the Gospel of Matthew where Jesus speaks of those separated from God in eternity being sent to "outer darkness."[55]

---

52. Lewis, *Collected Letters*, 2:640.

53. Lewis, *Best of C. S. Lewis*, 8.

54. Lewis, *Collected Letters*, 2:710.

55. Matthew 8:12; 22:13; 25:30.

Whether the "gap" that had opened between Lewis and Arthur at the end of the decade is attributed to Lewis accumulating new friends, or his burgeoning popularity, or the theological differences that had developed between them, or some combination of all these factors, a bridge across the gap was laid by Lewis's visit to Ireland to see Arthur in 1947. It was the first time the two friends saw each other since 1938. This trip to see Arthur would be the first in what would become semi-regular summer visits back to Ireland to see his friend and it would be the beginning of closing the gap between them.

CHAPTER 8

The Sword of Damocles

AFTER JACK LEWIS'S TRIP back to Ireland in 1947, there was a long eighteen-month gap in his correspondence with Arthur. What restarted the flow of letters was Lewis receiving news from his childhood friend Jane McNeil that Arthur's mother had passed away. Lewis then made plans to return to Ireland to see Arthur that summer. A vacation was just what the doctor ordered, literally. In June, Warnie had been away for a few days, and when he returned he found an ambulance at the Kilns. He recorded in his diary that Jack was "a very sick man when I went in to see him"[1] and that Humphrey Havard, Lewis's doctor and fellow Inkling, had diagnosed him as suffering from exhaustion. Havard's prescription, according to Warnie, was "a good holiday away from the Kilns."[2]

At home convalescing, Lewis writes Arthur, "I have been ill and am ordered real change. I am coming home (Belfast) for a month."[3] Lewis made plans to travel to Ireland on July 4 but ultimately his plans would be thwarted. The exhaustion that forced his hospitalization was the result of two factors. Cancelling his trip to Ireland was the result of one of those factors. Warren Lewis had always been a heavy drinker, but in recent years it had manifested itself with episodes of binge drinking, reaching the point

1. Lewis, *Collected Letters*, 2:943.
2. Lewis, *Collected Letters*, 2:944.
3. Lewis, *Collected Letters*, 2:945.

where he needed to be hospitalized during a 1947 trip to Ireland. Warnie was certainly aware of his demons and in the spring of 1949, shortly before his brother's hospitalization with exhaustion, noted in his diary, "I emerged from the Acland yesterday morning, where I had been as a finale to the wearisome cycle of insomnia – drugs – depression – spirits – illness."[4]

Jack was ever wary that Warnie could slip into one of his alcoholic stupors, and right after writing to Arthur about his plans to arrive on July 4 Warnie suffered another setback with his drinking that required hospitalization and eventually a few days in an asylum.[5] This forced Lewis to cancel his much-needed vacation in Ireland. It is here that Lewis confides to Arthur for public purposes he would tell the world Warnie's issues are related to "nervous insomnia" but that "in reality (this is for yr. private ear) it is Drink."[6]

Warnie quickly recovered enough for Lewis to reconsider his trip to visit Arthur, but the specter of Warnie's alcoholism hovered over his plans. The thought of having to cancel again weighed on Lewis: "I am in agony of hopes & fears as you may imagine."[7] A few days later, Warnie decided to take a trip on his own, and Lewis, fearing for his unsupervised brother, writes to Arthur that he "must be on duty," forcing him to permanently cancel the trip to visit Arthur.[8]

The letters from a decade earlier between Arthur and C. S. Lewis reflect theological differences. But during this time of Warnie's deepening alcoholism, the letters reflect a tenderness between friends and more theological unity. Lewis expresses gratitude for one of Arthur's "comforting" letters, telling him that it was "like a touch of a friend's hand in a dark place,"[9] while also reminding himself, "Don't imagine I doubt for a moment that what God sends us must be sent in love and will all be for the best if we have the

4. Lewis, *Collected Letters*, 2:922.

5. Lewis, *Collected Letters*, 2:953.

6. Lewis, *Collected Letters*, 2:952.

7. Lewis, *Collected Letters*, 2:959.

8. Lewis, *Collected Letters*, 2:960.

9. Lewis, *Collected Letters*, 2:952.

grace to use it so."[10] Lewis admits that he can intellectually assent to such a proposition, but his emotional assent is sometimes problematic. This admission by Lewis is part of what makes his letters to Arthur so valuable in that each one of us can identify with how Lewis was feeling. Biblical principles and concepts can seem distant and cold, and Lewis was struggling with the proposition that somehow God would use the consequences of Warnie's behavior for his purposes. Saint Paul tells us in Romans 8:28 that "all things work together for good,"[11] with the "all" encompassing both the good and bad. Lewis, like the rest of us, was learning to internalize this reality on a practical and daily basis.

The second contributing factor leading to Lewis's hospitalization from exhaustion was the physical and emotional condition of Janie Moore. Just as there seems to have been a calm in Warnie's episodic drinking, Lewis wrote Arthur in May of 1950 that he had to permanently place Mrs. Moore in a nursing home and that he would be unable to consider any further trips to visit him in Ireland.[12] This situation had been coming to a head for a while. Several years earlier, Lewis wrote Arthur that Mrs. Moore's condition made it such that "I cannot leave home for more than a night, or two at the outside, now. And this seems likely to be so as long as poor Minto lives."[13]

Compounding the emotional strain of placing her in a nursing home was what Lewis perceived to be "the crushing expense."[14] He told Arthur he was concerned with how the nursing home expenses would impact his ability to retire should Mrs. Moore live that long. In reality, Lewis's writings had made him very comfortable financially, yet his personal expenses were always marked by frugality and a generous spirit. So much so that in 1942 he had Owen Barfield establish a charitable trust known as the "Agape

10. Lewis, *Collected Letters*, 2:953.

11. Romans 8:28.

12. Lewis, *Collected Letters*, 3:28.

13. Lewis, *Collected Letters*, 2:709.

14. Lewis, *Collected Letters*, 3:28.

Fund," where two-thirds of Lewis's royalties from writing would be placed for him to distribute at his discretion.

Prior to Janie Moore's placement in the nursing home, her arthritis had immobilized her and her decreasing mental capacity brought on by advancing dementia had produced a toxic environment at the Kilns. Lewis details how bad things were on the home front in a letter to Mary Van Deusen: "Strictly between ourselves, I have lived most of it (that is now over) in a house wh. was hardly ever at peace for 24 hours, amidst senseless wranglings, lyings, backbitings, follies, and *scares*. I never went home without a feeling of terror as to what appalling situation might have developed in my absence."[15]

For his part, it appears Arthur tried to provide his friend with comfort during this time, as Lewis thanks Arthur for encouraging him to remember Christ's exhortation in Matthew 6, using the examples of "the birds of the air" and "the lilies of the field,"[16] to not be anxious about our lives. Lewis responds to Arthur that "I *do* try to consider the lilies of the field'" but the difficult part is that while his reason understands the concept, "my *nerves* do not always obey it!"[17] Janie Moore's move from the Kilns into a nursing home did not eliminate all of Lewis's stress. He dutifully visited her each day, telling Arthur that the visits "are v. grievous to me."[18]

But with her out of the home, he was now free to spend some time on self-care, telling Arthur he was getting more exercise by swimming in the River Cherwell. With Mrs. Moore gone, the Kilns also became more hospitable to guests, or as Lewis tells Arthur, "less horrible to stay in than I know it was before,"[19] and Lewis used the opportunity to invite Arthur for a visit.

Janie Moore passed away on January 12, 1951, marking the end of a dark period in Lewis's life. Warnie's drinking coupled with the decline of Mrs. Moore produced a constant swirling vortex of

15. Lewis, *Collected Letters*, 3:108.
16. Verses 26 and 28, respectively.
17. Lewis, *Collected Letters*, 3:29.
18. Lewis, *Collected Letters*, 3:37.
19. Lewis, *Collected Letters*, 3:37.

domestic oppression of Lewis, who tells his friend Owen Barfield, "Dog stools and human vomits have made day to day: one of those days when you feel at 11 a.m. that it really must be 3 p.m."[20] But, much like the early years of the Second World War, when Lewis's life consisted of similar domestic and personal upheaval, this period in his life was also marked by astonishing productivity. Though not published until 1955, Lewis began writing his autobiography, *Surprised by Joy*, while also continuing his work on the magisterial, yet forensic, *English Literature in the Sixteenth Century, Excluding Drama*, a project begun in 1935 and not brought to publication until 1954. More importantly, it was during this unhappy and chaotic period in his life that Lewis embarked in earnest on what would be his most enduring legacy. Born from a picture in Lewis's head of a "Faun carrying an umbrella"[21] when he was sixteen years old, that image would germinate into pictures and dreams of lions, eventually culminating with the Chronicles of Narnia. The conception of each of the seven Narnian books began with Lewis seeing a picture in his head and then saying to himself, "'Let's try to make a story about it.'"[22]

When Lewis sent Owen Barfield the note complaining that his days were filled with dog stools and human vomit in 1949, he was also knee-deep in bringing to life the story of what happened when a young girl named Lucy Pevensie stepped into a wardrobe while staying at an eccentric old professor's home. Perhaps the creative process served as an escape from his domestic prison, but, whatever it was, by the end of the year he had completed both *The Lion, the Witch and the Wardrobe* and *Prince Caspian*. In the very same letter that Lewis tells Arthur how grievous his visits to Mrs. Moore are, he tells Arthur to be on the lookout for "a children's story" that he will soon have published.[23] *The Lion, the Witch and the Wardrobe* was published in 1950 with *Prince Caspian* published in 1951. In 1950, Lewis finished writing *The Voyage of the Dawn*

20. Lewis, *Collected Letters*, 2:929.
21. Lewis, *Of Other Worlds*, 42.
22. Lewis, *Of Other Worlds*, 42.
23. Lewis, *Collected Letters*, 3:38.

Treader and *The Horse and His Boy*. In 1951, he finished *The Silver Chair* and a good portion of *The Magician's Nephew*. Lewis interrupted his work on the Narnian stories to complete *English Literature in the Sixteenth Century* and then returned to write *The Last Battle*, finishing it by March of 1953. He put the final touches on *The Magician's Nephew* in early 1954, completing the Chronicles of Narnia in an amazing burst of imaginative output.

With Mrs. Moore's death, the doors to Lewis's domestic prison swung open and he found himself with a newfound freedom. This is reflected in his letter to Arthur informing him of Mrs. Moore's death, where he writes, "Minto died a fortnight ago. Please pray for her soul," and then, exercising his new freedom, he quickly transitions to, "Wd. it suit you if I arrived at your local inn on Sat. March 31st and left on Mon. April 16?"[24] This trip to see Arthur began a streak of five consecutive years where Lewis would be able to take a vacation to Ireland to visit his friend. These visits back to his roots seem to have recharged Lewis's batteries. After his trip in 1952, he writes Arthur, "I've got a 100 Horsepower cold but feel mentally & spiritually much the better from our holiday. It – and you – have done me lots of good."[25]

The year 1952 would be a pivotal one for Lewis. The BBC talks he had delivered during the Second World War had been published in three small books: *Broadcast Talks*, published in 1942, *Christian Behaviour*, published in 1943, and *Beyond Personality*, published in 1944. *Mere Christianity*, published in 1952, was a compilation of all three, with Lewis adding some additional content. 1952 was also the year Lewis met Helen Gresham. The front door to entering Lewis's life was, as for so many of Lewis's most important relationships, the medium of a letter. Warnie Lewis remembered, "Until 10 January 1950 neither of us had ever heard of her; then she appeared in the mail as just another American fan, Mrs. W.L. Gresham from the neighborhood in New York."[26]

24. Lewis, *Collected Letters*, 3:90.
25. Lewis, *Collected Letters*, 3:226.
26. Dorsett, *And God Came In*, 70.

Born Helen Joy Davidman, at the time she wrote Lewis, she was married to the American writer Bill Gresham, whom she met while working for the communist periodical *New Masses*. They had two children together: David, born in 1944, and Douglas, born in 1945. It was an unhappy marriage, as Bill was unfaithful to Joy through a series of affairs, and physically abusive to both Joy and the boys. She had settled on atheism at eight years old: "I believed in nothing. Men, I said were only apes. Virtue only custom. Life is only an electromechanical reaction."[27] Like so many people before her, she began reading Lewis and then converted to Christianity, along with her husband.[28] In the Gospel of Matthew, Jesus tells a parable about a sower sowing seeds. Some seeds were consumed by birds, some seeds sprung up quickly but were scorched by the sun because they had no roots, and some seeds grew but were choked by thorns, yet "Other seeds fell on good soil and produced grain."[29] Joy's faith took root and continued to grow. Sadly, it appears Bill's faith suffered the fate of other seeds in Jesus's parable as he soon drifted into Scientology.[30]

While the early letters between Joy Gresham and C. S. Lewis have not survived, we can get a flavor for Lewis's response to Joy's initial letter to Lewis from a letter she wrote to Chad Walsh in January of 1950. Joy had been communicating with Walsh, who penned the first book-length biography of Lewis in 1949, titled *C. S. Lewis: Apostle to the Skeptics*. Joy told Walsh, "Just got a letter from Lewis in the mail. I think I told you I'd raised an argument or two on some points? Lord, he knocked my props out from under me unerringly: one shot to a pigeon. I haven't a scrap of case left. And, what's more, I've seldom enjoyed anything more."[31]

While her faith was growing, her marriage to Bill Gresham was collapsing. Bill struggled with alcoholism, anger, and infidelity. To compound their domestic turmoil, Joy's first cousin, Renee

27. King, ed., *Out of My Bone*, 86.
28. Hooper, *C. S. Lewis*, 59.
29. Matthew 13:8.
30. Hooper, *C. S. Lewis*, 60.
31. Dorsett, *And God Came In*, 70.

Pierce, who was having marital troubles of her own, moved in with Bill and Joy.[32] Seeking clarity, Joy sought an escape and so she traveled to England with one goal—to meet C. S. Lewis, the man whose writings had been so instrumental in her spiritual growth. In her communications with Chad Walsh, Walsh assured her that Lewis was approachable and kind-hearted, easing any apprehension she had about visiting Lewis. She had an existing friend living in London at the time, Phyllis Williams, who had agreed to let Joy stay with her. The time away in England would give her the opportunity to complete a book she had begun, which Lewis would eventually contribute the introduction to, *Smoke on the Mountain: An Interpretation of the Ten Commandments*.

Upon her arrival, Joy and Williams invited Lewis to lunch at the Eastgate Hotel, located just a few yards from Magdalen College. While we don't know the tone, tenor, or substance of the conversation at that initial meeting, it must have gone well enough that Lewis reciprocated by inviting Joy and Williams to lunch with him at Magdalen a few days later. Lewis's friend and biographer George Sayer was present and records in his Lewis biography that the conversation ranged from New York City skyscrapers, to modern American literature, to the overindulgence of alcohol at American luncheons.[33] Lewis was amused by her anti-American sentiments. When he mentioned he came from farming stock on his father's side of the family, Joy responded with the very forward, if not overtly flirtatious, "I felt that . . . Where else could you get the vitality?"[34]

Another lunch followed, this time with Warnie present. Joy lacked a proper English filter and Warnie recorded of the luncheon that she "turned to me in the presence of three or four men, and asked in the most natural tone in the world, 'Is there anywhere in this monastic establishment where a lady can relieve herself?'"[35]

---

32. Hooper, *C. S. Lewis*, 60.
33. Sayer, *Jack*, 353.
34. Sayer, *Jack*, 353.
35. Hooper, *C. S. Lewis*, 61.

Joy's New York manners were not an impediment to a developing friendship with Lewis, as he invited her to spend some time at the Kilns over Christmas with him and Warnie. Lewis was concerned that he and Warnie would have to alter their holiday routine of walking tours to local pubs to drink and consume bread and cheese. Instead, Joy fit right in, with Warnie remembering, "We treated her just as if she was a man. She loved the pubs. Walked fairly well considering that she was not used to it, drank her pints of beer and often made us laugh."[36] Lewis also looked over her manuscript for *Smoke on the Mountain* during this time.

It would not be a stretch to say that by this time Joy had developed an emotional attachment to Lewis. Her own marriage had completely disintegrated, as while she was staying at the Kilns she received a letter from Bill informing her that he had fallen in love with Renee, as Renee was more interested in focusing on meeting the needs of a husband and children.[37] Bill suggested that the best solution for all involved would be for him to marry Renee, for Joy to marry "some swell guy," and for everyone to live in close proximity for the sake of David and Douglas.[38] When Joy showed Lewis this letter, he advised her to divorce Bill. Despite Warnie's reflections of a fine time being had by all over the Christmas break, it appears that Lewis had reached a breaking point with the length of Joy's stay, telling his godson, Laurence Harwood, "I am completely 'circumvented' by a guest, asked for one week but staying for three, who talks from morning till night. I hope you'll have a nicer Christmas than I. I can't write (write? I can hardly think or breath. I can't believe it's all real)."[39]

Despite ending the year with a houseguest that had overstayed her welcome, Lewis told Arthur that it had been the happiest year of his life.[40] Joy returned to the United States to start the process of divorce with Bill. Upon her arrival back in New York,

36. Sayer, *Jack*, 353.
37. Lewis, *Collected Letters*, 3:275.
38. Lewis, *Collected Letters*, 3:275.
39. Lewis, *Collected Letters*, 3:268.
40. Lewis, *Collected Letters*, 3:234.

she wrote to Chad Walsh that she was resolved to begin her new life in England with the boys once she finished the restructuring of her personal and financial life that always accompanies the process of divorce.[41] She was able to return to London and set up residence in an apartment the following November, and was then back at the Kilns, bringing David and Douglas to meet Lewis, in mid-December. Prior to meeting Lewis, the boys had read *The Lion, the Witch and the Wardrobe* and formed a preconceived vision of what its author would look like. For eight-year-old Douglas, that first meeting would be deflating.

> Aha! Here they are. Here they are! The voice came from a slightly stooped round-shouldered balding gentleman whose full smiling mouth revealed long, prominent teeth, yellowed, like those of some large rodent, by tobacco staining. He was wearing the oddest clothes, too! Baggy grey flannel trousers dusty with cigarette ash and sagging at the turn-ups (equally full of ash), an old tweed jacket with the elbows worn away, an open, soft collared shirt, which had once, in all probability, been white and backless black leather slippers (in fact, they had backs, but over the years they had been trodden flat, for he ever only thrust his feet into them, and never actually put them on).[42]

Young Douglas was terribly disappointed. After all, "Here was a man who was on speaking terms with King Peter, with the great Lion, Aslan himself. Here was a man who had been to Narnia; surely he could at least wear a silver chain mail and be girt about with a jewel-encrusted sword-belt. This was the heroic figure of whom Mother has so often spoken?"[43]

Joy was not the only one undergoing significant change. Lewis would experience a major change too, as to his employment. In 1954, after some arm-twisting by Tolkien, Lewis accepted an offer from Cambridge University to become Professor of Medieval

41. Dorsett, *And God Came In*, 94.

42. Gresham, *Lenten Lands*, 55.

43. Gresham, *Lenten Lands*, 55.

and Renaissance Literature despite Lewis's original apprehension at starting over somewhere new. This apprehension is reflected in one of his letters to Arthur: "Yes: the move looms large and black – all the things to 'see to' and all the decisions to make."[44] Cambridge happily accommodated Lewis by allowing him commute home to Oxford during the weekends. While Lewis's home would remain in Oxford, in August of 1955 it became home for Joy and the boys as well, as they moved to Headington, a suburb on the outskirts of the city. Separated now by just one mile, Lewis and Joy were able to spend increasingly more time together. The trajectory of their relationship seemed to observers such as Warnie and Chad Walsh to be heading in one direction—marriage.[45] Joy had told friends she was in love with Lewis, but Lewis seems to have held his cards closer to the vest. Plus, the fact that Joy had been previously married—her divorce was finalized on August 5, 1954, with Bill turning right around and marrying Renee the very same day—was a significant impediment for Lewis.

Once settled in Oxford, Joy had trouble getting her passport renewed so that she could remain in England. This may have been a result of her ties to communism earlier in her life. Whatever the status of their relationship at that time, Lewis did not want Joy and the boys to return to the United States. He had a solution, one that he had been contemplating for a while, and one that he had to this point only discussed with Arthur, most likely during his two weeks with Arthur in Ireland in September of 1955. The following month, on October 30, 1955, Lewis writes Arthur, "The other affair remains where it did. I don't feel the point about a 'false position'. Everyone whom it concerned wd. be told. The 'reality' wd. be, from my point of view, adultery and therefore mustn't happen. (An easy resolution when one doesn't in the least want it!)."[46]

While we do not know specifically what Arthur pressed Lewis on regarding Lewis's plan to keep Joy in the country, the "false position" the two discussed was almost certainly Lewis suggesting

44. Lewis, *Collected Letters*, 3:537.

45. Dorsett, *And God Came In*, 114.

46. Lewis, *Collected Letters*, 3:669.

he could marry Joy in a civil marriage solely for the purpose of her obtaining English citizenship, versus the "reality" of a Christian marriage with Joy, which would have constituted adultery in the eyes of the Anglican Church. Some might be surprised to know that Lewis held a bifurcated view of marriage, one civil and one Christian. However, this is a view he clearly expresses in *Mere Christianity*, writing, "There ought to be two distinct kinds of marriage: one governed by the State with rules enforced on all citizens, the other governed by the Church with rule enforced by her on her own members."[47] Not only did Lewis believe in two distinct forms of marriage, but he believed the contrast between the two should be visible to the entire world: "The distinction ought to be quite sharp, so that a man knows which couples are married in a Christian sense and which are not."[48]

Does Lewis's bifurcated view water down the sanctity or concept of marriage? Lewis viewed it the other way round, in that by distinguishing between a civil marriage and a Christian marriage, he was elevating marriage to its proper place for those who take seriously Christ's teaching that a man and a woman "shall become one flesh,"[49] and distilling out those who do not. The idea of marrying Joy in a civil ceremony would solve the matter of allowing her and the boys to remain in the country, and yet, in Lewis's mind, they would not be married in the Christian sense and would only have entered into a civil contract. On April 23, 1956, he and Joy were married in a civil service at the Oxford Registry Office with Humphrey Havard and Austin Farrer serving as witnesses. Lewis then boarded the train to return to his teaching duties at Cambridge and Joy returned to her home in Headington.

Lewis sought to keep this arrangement with Joy quiet. He never mentioned it in his correspondence with Arthur until he was forced to, finally revealing it to him and the rest of the world because of Joy being diagnosed with cancer.[50] One evening, Joy

47. Lewis, *Mere Christianity*, 112.
48. Lewis, *Mere Christianity*, 112.
49. Matthew 19:5.
50. Lewis, *Collected Letters*, 3:812.

went to answer a telephone call from Austin Farrer's wife, Katharine, and tripped over the telephone wire, snapping her femur, which had been weakened by the presence of cancer. Subsequent treatment revealed cancer in advanced stages in other areas of her body.[51] Lewis sought to bring her to the Kilns, and, as he wrote Arthur, "in order to avoid scandal" he needed to reveal to the public that they were married.[52] So on Christmas Eve 1956 an announcement was placed in *The Times*: "A marriage has taken place between Professor C. S. Lewis of Magdalene College Cambridge, and Mrs. Joy Gresham, now a patient in the Churchill Hospital, Oxford. It is requested that no letters be sent."[53]

Joy's prognosis was subsequently relayed to Arthur: "Joy has now been sent home from the hospital, not because she is better but because they can do nothing for her."[54] While Joy's condition seemed irreversible, there had been a reversal in Lewis's feelings for Joy. It is difficult to pinpoint when Lewis's affections turned romantic, but as Joy seemingly lay dying of cancer, Lewis sought the sacrament of Christian marriage for them. His first appeal was to the bishop of Oxford. Lewis felt that he had discovered a theological loophole. Bill Gresham had been married prior to meeting Joy. When he and Joy were married, Bill's first wife was still alive, thus invalidating Joy and Bill's marriage, meaning that a Christian marriage between he and Joy would be the first for each. The bishop denied Lewis's request as the Anglican Church recognized civil marriages and in the eyes of the Church he and Joy were already married.

After the bishop refused Lewis's request for the sacrament of Christian marriage, Lewis invited a former student, now Anglican priest, Peter Bide, to come to Oxford and pray for Joy and her healing. While Bide was there to lay hands on Joy, Lewis surprised him by telling him that the bishop and Lewis's own parish priest had refused to marry them, and then asked Bide, "Peter, I know this isn't

51. McGrath, *C. S. Lewis*, 333.

52. Lewis, *Collected Letters*, 3:812.

53. Lewis, *Collected Letters*, 3:818.

54. Lewis, *Collected Letters*, 3:842.

fair, but do you think you could marry us?"[55] Bide asked for some time alone to think on it. Through his thought process, "In the end there seemed only one Court of Appeal. I asked myself what He would have done and that somehow finished the argument."[56] Peter Bide married Joy Gresham and C. S. Lewis the very next day, March 27, 1957.

Even though Joy and Lewis were able to receive the sacrament of Christian marriage, Lewis reached a nadir in his life as his own health was beginning to deteriorate. During the summer, he informed Arthur he had been diagnosed with osteoporosis, a condition where his bones were becoming brittle as a result of calcium deficiency, and he was forced to sleep with a board under his mattress.[57] Warnie was again hospitalized from an alcoholic binge and had just told Lewis he had been diagnosed with a heart condition, leaving him a year to live. This confluence of his own oncoming illness, Warnie's alcoholism, and Joy's life-threatening cancer caused Lewis to live his daily existence in an exhausted haze, telling Arthur, ". . . when life gets very bad (do you find?) a sort of anaesthesia sets in."[58]

Joy was released from the hospital and returned to the Kilns, with the prognosis that she would live only for matter of weeks, maybe months. Astonishingly, instead of dying, she began to recover. Just three months after Lewis's initial dire report to Arthur, Lewis is able to tell Arthur that "Joy's improvement has gone beyond anything we'd dare hope and she can now (limping, of course, and with a stick) get about the house and the garden."[59] His osteoporosis also improved and Warnie's heart condition was found to not be fatal, but merely a byproduct of his alcoholism. This undulation in his and Joy's circumstances made it possible for them to begin living their lives like newlyweds, which included the prospect of taking a trip to Ireland to see Arthur.

55. Hooper, *C. S. Lewis*, 634.
56. Hooper, *C. S. Lewis*, 634.
57. Lewis, *Collected Letters*, 3:878.
58. Lewis, *Collected Letters*, 3:878.
59. Lewis, *Collected Letters*, 3:900.

As Joy improved, Lewis was cautious about making plans too far out, telling Arthur that "the sword of Damocles hangs over us."[60] Lewis was alluding to the story told by Cicero of what happened when a courtier named Damocles was able to switch places with the king, Dionysius. Damocles was suddenly presented with everything he had ever wanted, but Dionysius had hung a sword tied with just a single horse's hair over the throne where Damocles now sat. Living with the prosect of the sword hanging precariously over his head was too much for Damocles and he begged to switch positions back with the king. For Lewis, the prospect of Joy's cancer returning was like the sword of Damocles, always hovering over their heads.

Time is a precious commodity, and each of us is allotted only a certain portion. For the time being, Joy had enough of a reserve to permit a trip to Ireland in July of 1958. Rather than risk jarring her bones via ship while crossing the Irish Sea, Lewis and Joy both boarded a plane for the first time. Lewis was excited at the prospect of his lifelong friend meeting Joy for the first time and wondered who would do most of the talking as the three traveled the Irish countryside in Arthur's car, finally concluding, "Actually, against you *and* her I shd. have no chance."[61] The trip was such a success that it was repeated the following year. In anticipation, Joy wrote Arthur, "I'll be a surprise to you this year – I can walk a mile without tiring, now! I hope you feel as well as it do."[62]

Joy's reprieve from cancer ended shortly after this second trip to Ireland. Despite telling Arthur she felt so well, by October that single horse's hair holding the sword of Damocles broke, and a visit to the doctor for a checkup revealed that her cancer had returned. Lewis informed Arthur of this development in March of 1960, telling him, "The doctors hold out no hope of a cure; it is only a question of how soon the end comes and how painful it will be."[63] But there was still one more trip for Lewis and Joy to

---

60. Lewis, *Collected Letters*, 3:925.
61. Lewis, *Collected Letters*, 3:931.
62. Lewis, *They Stand Together*, 552.
63. Lewis, *Collected Letters*, 3:1139.

make. Lewis told Arthur that they hoped to take a trip to Greece, and in April of 1960 they flew with their friends Roger and June Lancelyn Green for a tour of the country. Recalling the trip, Lewis told Walter Hooper just before his own death, "Joy knew she was dying, I knew she was dying – and *she* knew *I* knew she was dying – but when we heard the shepherds playing their flutes in the hills it seemed to make no difference!"[64]

The temporal parting of Jack and Joy Lewis occurred July 13, 1960. Lewis wrote Arthur describing Joy's last hours, telling him that though she was lucid when awake, "There were a couple of hours of atrocious pain."[65] Lewis also revealed to Arthur two of Joy's last intimate comments, "You have made me very happy" and "I am at peace with God."[66]

Joy's death sent Lewis into a grieving tailspin. To find his way out, he followed the advice given by one of his favorite writers, Jane Austen, in *Mansfield Park*: "There is nothing like employment, active indispensable employment, for relieving sorrow."[67] Like he had done in other periods of despair and darkness throughout his life, Lewis picked up his pen. For strictly therapeutic purposes, Lewis spelled out the emotional trajectory of his grieving process in just a few short weeks after Joy passed away. He showed the manuscript to his friend Roger Lancelyn Green, who had accompanied him and Joy on their trip to Greece, and was convinced to publish it.[68] Not wanting to alarm his friends, Lewis published *A Grief Observed*, which continues to comfort so many others enduring the grieving process, under the pen name N. W. Clerk. Simultaneously to writing *A Grief Observed*, Lewis was also writing *An Experiment in Criticism*, also published in 1961, and reworking his poems with an eye toward publishing them in the future.

A welcomed interlude in Lewis's productivity during 1961 was a letter from Arthur in June. Arthur wrote to say he was going

64. Lewis, *They Stand Together*, 553.

65. Lewis, *Collected Letters*, 3:1181.

66. Lewis, *Collected Letters*, 3:1181.

67. Austen, *Mansfield Park*, 401.

68. Hooper, *C. S. Lewis*, 196.

to be in London and wondered if he could come to Oxford for a visit.[69] Lewis writes back, "Your letter has brightened my whole sky."[70] The friends spent two days together at the Kilns, with Lewis telling Arthur in a post-visit letter, "Our little re-union was one of the happiest times I've had for many a long day."[71] It would be the last time the two saw each other alive.

69. Lewis, *They Stand Together*, 555.
70. Lewis, *Collected Letters*, vol.3, 1263.
71. Lewis, *Collected Letters*, vol.3, 1278.

CHAPTER 9

Conclusion

As Arthur Greeves arrived at the Kilns for a two-day visit with his oldest friend, C. S. Lewis, in May 1961, both were struggling with significant physical ailments, and each was sensing the limits of his own mortality. A few days before this last visit, Lewis responded to a letter from Arthur, who had recently complained of his heart condition, observing, "The party gets thinner and I suppose you and I shall be leaving it soon."[1] A few days later, in a letter that has survived, Arthur elaborated on his condition, writing of "HEART GROGGINESS," including palpitations and breathlessness, while also answering Lewis's comment about the party thinning out, writing, "Yes, I wonder how much longer? Aren't I four years older?"[2] Arthur observed Lewis's poor health during their time together. In the margins of a letter Arthur received just after this last visit, he wrote, "He was looking very ill."[3]

For the remaining two years of his life, Lewis's health would spiral downwards. In his first letter to Arthur after their visit, Lewis tells Arthur he will be going into the hospital for an operation on "an enlarged prostate gland."[4] But once he entered the Acland Nursing Home, the doctors determined that his deteriorating

1. Lewis, *Collected Letters*, 3:1263.
2. Lewis, *Collected Letters*, 3:1266.
3. Lewis, *They Stand Together*, 559.
4. Lewis, *Collected Letters*, 3:1277.

heart and kidneys would not allow them to operate. Instead, his prostate condition would require him to wear a catheter, and his other medical issues would need to be monitored.

His deteriorating physical condition resulted in Lewis not being able to travel to Cambridge to teach for a period of time. The catheter proved to be problematic, about which he noted to Arthur, "I need to be near a life-line (the plumbing often goes wrong.)"[5] Nearly a year later, however, his condition had stabilized and he was able to return to Cambridge in April of 1962 to deliver lectures on Spenser's *Faerie Queene*.[6] Lewis updated Arthur on his condition from a letter during this period, writing, "Some months ago they had decided that I should never be ripe for that operation but must just carry on, always wearing a catheter, on a low protein diet, and being careful about stairs. They let me go up to Cambridge at the beginning of last term, reluctantly, and 'as an experiment'. The experiment has however been a far greater success than was hoped and I am now definitely better than I have been since the trouble began."[7]

Toward the end of 1962, Lewis was feeling well enough that he could consider making a trip, along with his stepson Douglas, who would carry his bags, to Ireland to visit Arthur. By March of 1963 they had formalized their plan to be together, along with Douglas, from July 28 through August 12. Lewis's excitement is evident in closing out a March 22 letter with, "We're both too old to let our remaining chances slip!"[8]

Sadly, this visit was not to be. Lewis was forced to cancel his visit with Arthur, writing on July 11, "I have had a collapse as regards the heart trouble and the holiday has to be cancelled . . . I don't mind – or not much – missing the jaunt, but it is a blow missing *you*. Bless you."[9] A few days after writing this letter to Arthur, he went back to the Acland Nursing Home to be examined

5. Lewis, *Collected Letters*, 3:1352.
6. McGrath, *C. S. Lewis*, 350.
7. Lewis, *Collected Letters*, 3:1352.
8. Lewis, *Collected Letters*, 3:1418.
9. Lewis, *Collected Letters*, 3:1440.

and while there he suffered a heart attack. After he lapsed into a coma, his condition was considered serious enough that Lewis was given the rite of extreme unction, or last rights.[10] Remarkably, an hour later Lewis woke from the coma and requested a cup of tea.[11]

Lewis returned home to the Kilns on August 6.[12] Warnie had been in Ireland since June, anticipating the now-aborted trip to see Arthur, and had not returned, most likely having relapsed into a drunken stupor. In C. S. Lewis's last letter to Arthur Greeves, he discusses having been in a coma in July and expresses regret that he came out of it: "I mean, having been gilded so painlessly up to the Gate it seems hard to have had it shut in one's face and know that the whole process must some day be gone thro' again, and perhaps far less pleasantly! Poor Lazarus! But God knows best."[13]

Lewis also describes to Arthur his anguish regarding Warnie: "W., meanwhile has completely deserted me. He has been in Ireland since June and doesn't even write, and is, I suppose, drinking himself to death. He has of course been fully informed of my condition and more than one friend or more has written him strong appeals but without the slightest result."[14] Fortunately, Lewis was not alone. He was being cared for by a male nurse, Alec Ross, his gardener, Fred Paxford (after whom Lewis modeled Puddleglum the Marshwiggle in *The Silver Chair*), and his housekeeper, Molly Miller.

Thirty-three years before this final letter to Arthur, C. S. Lewis had written a letter to Arthur discussing their friendship, where he says, "Secondly, there are a great many subjects on which you are the only person whom I can write to or be written to by with full understanding. Thirdly our common ground represents what is really (I think) the deepest stratum of my life, the thing in me that, if there should be another personal life, is most likely to survive the dissolution of my brain. Certainly when I come to die

10. Lewis, *Collected Letters*, 3:1446.
11. Lewis, *Collected Letters*, 3:1446.
12. McGrath, *C. S. Lewis*, 356.
13. Lewis, *Collected Letters*, 3:1456.
14. Lewis, *Collected Letters*, 3:1455.

I am more likely to remember certain things that you and I have explored or suffered or enjoyed together than anything else."[15] Now just a few weeks before his death from renal failure and cardiac degeneration on November 22, 1963, Lewis's prophecy about remembering Arthur on his death bed was being fulfilled. His last words to Arthur, "But oh Arthur, never to see you again!"[16] are dripping with anguish, bringing to its sad culmination a friendship spanning almost fifty years.

Though he died nearly seventy years ago, C. S. Lewis is still teaching us today, especially regarding the subject of friendship, and his relationship with Arthur Greeves serves as the syllabus. In his book *The Four Loves*, Lewis laments that the modern world places so little value on friendship because so very few actually experience it. Sadly, seventy years later, not much has changed. For many people the words "friend" and "friendship" have been diluted to the point where a person can have thousands of "friends" by sending and accepting friend requests on Facebook or other social media without ever meeting another person or hearing the sound of another's voice. It's not hard to imagine what Lewis would think of friend requests or followers in our world of social media today considering that he writes in *Surprised by Joy*, "acquaintance or general society has always meant little to me, and I cannot quite understand why a man should wish to know more people than he can make real friends of."[17]

Friendship on social media requires keeping up appearances, projecting and constructing an image of a successful and happy life rooted in the desire for personal affirmation and "likes." Conversely, the C. S. Lewis–Arthur Greeves friendship was rooted in vulnerability. Vulnerability is a scarcity in our contemporary world because it is associated with weakness. In making the distinction between friendship and *eros*, Lewis writes, "Eros will have naked bodies, Friendship naked personalities."[18] In a friendship

15. Lewis, *Collected Letters*, 1:916.
16. Lewis, *Collected Letters*, 3:1456.
17. Lewis, *Surprised by Joy*, 32–33.
18. Lewis, *Four Loves*, 71.

like the one between C. S. Lewis and Arthur Greeves, both parties submit and consent to be known, revealing the nakedness of their authentic selves, flaws and all, by letting down their guard and being vulnerable.

Perhaps the most glaring example of one person in a sense disrobing for the other during the course of this friendship was Arthur's revelation to Lewis that he was gay. In a 1918 letter, long before Lewis's conversion to Christianity, Lewis congratulates Arthur on having "the moral courage to form your own opinions independently, in defiance of the old taboos," with homosexuality being a "mystery only to be fully understood by those who are made that way."[19] The topic of sexuality appears numerous times throughout their correspondence, especially as young men. It is a popular topic among adolescent boys, and discussions between C. S. Lewis and Arthur Greeves were no different. The important point for our purposes is that Arthur felt safe within the confines of their friendship in telling C. S. Lewis he was gay, especially given that the laws in England at the time made homosexual acts criminal.

It's also important to note that after Lewis's conversion to Christianity there was no further discussion or commentary in his letters on Arthur's sexuality. Absence of evidence is not evidence of absence, and it would be unrealistic to believe that during the thousands of hours the two spent together over the course of their friendship the topic did not reemerge. Lewis's views on homosexuality, which are consistent with Scripture, are summed up in a letter to Sheldon Vanauken in 1954. Vanauken, who was teaching at Lynchburg College in Virginia at the time, was counseling some Christians who were same-sex attracted, and he had written to Lewis seeking advice.[20] In mapping "out the boundaries within which all discussion must go on," Lewis takes it for "certain that the *physical* satisfaction of the homosexual desires is a sin."[21] He writes that those with same-sex attraction must abstain from

19. Lewis, *Collected Letters*, 1:371.
20. Lewis, *Collected Letters*, 3:471.
21. Lewis, *Collected Letters*, 3:471.

acting upon their desires just as an unmarried heterosexual person must abstain from acting on theirs. Yet, through the "tribulation" of abstinence, those who struggle with same-sex attraction can turn it to "spiritual gain."[22] Lewis refers to a letter he had received from a gay man, a letter that Lewis destroyed in an attempt to be discreet, which indicated that his same-sex attraction had led to a "sympathy and understanding" that heterosexual men and women cannot not provide, a view consistent with St. Paul's observation in 2 Corinthians 1:4, where he tells us that through our afflictions we are able to comfort those with similar afflictions.

Lewis's letter to Vanauken provides a teaching moment for contemporary believers, especially since one's view on all matters sexual is a dividing line, with those holding the orthodox view of marriage and sexuality being perceived as being on the wrong side of history. One important lesson Christians can learn from Lewis is his tone regarding homosexuality. Too often, modern Christianity has falsely given the impression that homosexuality is somehow in a super-class of sin all on its own. In fact, St. Paul in 1 Corinthians 6:9–10 includes it as just one in a laundry list, along with idolatry, adultery, thievery, greed, and drunkenness, that makes someone unrighteous and in danger of not inheriting the kingdom of God. Honest self-reflection places each of us at some point somewhere on this list. Still another lesson contemporary Christians can learn from Lewis is found in recognizing that Arthur's homosexuality was not a wedge that disqualified him from being not only just Lewis's friend, but his very best friend. It is obvious from Lewis's other writings that he was not affirming of homosexual behavior, yet this did not prohibit him from loving Arthur.

Vulnerability in a friendship is a two-way street and C. S. Lewis was as vulnerable with Arthur as Arthur was with him. He trusted Arthur with his most intimate and private thoughts. Early in their friendship, an adolescent Lewis confided in Arthur about his penchant for sadomasochism, about his fictional dalliance with a Belgian girl, and his first experience being drunk. As an adult,

22. Lewis, *Collected Letters*, 3:472.

Lewis confided in Arthur that pride was his "besetting sin."[23] Lewis once wrote Arthur that, while attempting his afternoon "meditations," he was horrified that "one out of every three is a thought of self-admiration . . . Depth under depth of self-love and self-admiration. Closely connected with this is the difficulty I find in making even the faintest approach to giving up my own will: which as everyone has told us is the only thing to do."[24]

Then, there is the letter to Arthur from 1930 on which Arthur had penciled at the top, "very private" and "to be burnt."[25] Only certain pages of the letter were destroyed and what remains of it picks up with, "have fallen so far below – MYSELF!!! . . . I hadn't meant to give you such a dose of myself – but there is hardly any of it that I can say to any one but you and it is a relief to let it out."[26] It's impossible to say with certainty what the contents of this letter contained, but it was serious enough that either Lewis or Arthur felt that it needed to be destroyed. Lewis's vulnerability with Arthur is evident here in a way that is not found in his relationship with anyone else. It was Arthur only who Lewis unveiled himself to by revealing whatever events made up the subject of the letter.

C. S. Lewis's friendship with Arthur Greeves also teaches us that friendship improves our quality of life by enhancing our happiness and joy. In *The Four Loves*, Lewis points out that, biologically, humanity "has no need of" friendship.[27] But even though "Friendship has no survival value," it is "one of those things that give value to survival."[28] Lewis was especially in his element when he was gathered around a fire with his friends, engaging in a rough-and-tumble linguistic give-and-take, or taking long walks with them through the countryside, stopping overnight at small-town inns. In our modern world, friendship is the very best antidote for the current epidemic of loneliness. Due to our advanced

23. Lewis, *Collected Letters*, 1:878.

24. Lewis, *Collected Letters*, 1:878.

25. Lewis, *Collected Letters*, 1:888.

26. Lewis, *Collected Letters*, 1:888.

27. Lewis, *Four Loves*, 58.

28. Lewis, *Collected Letters*, 1:878.

technology, it has never in history been easier to connect in some way with another person, via Facebook, Instagram, Skype, or email, and yet people are lonelier than ever. A recent national study by the insurance company Cigna found that almost half of all Americans sometimes or always feel lonely and that only 53 percent of Americans have meaningful in-person social interactions, such as having an extended conversation with a friend or spending quality time with family on a daily basis.[29] A study by the National Academies of Sciences, Engineering, and Medicine shows that loneliness is associated with higher rates of mortality, cognitive decline, and depression.[30] Deep and meaningful friendships, like those accumulated by Lewis over the course of his life, help stave off loneliness and provide happiness. For C. S. Lewis, friendship went far beyond being merely an antidote for loneliness; it was a wellspring of delight and joy. In a 1935 letter to Arthur, Lewis writes, "Friendship is the greatest of worldly goods. Certainly to me it is the chief happiness of life."[31]

Finally, the C. S. Lewis and Arthur Greeves relationship teaches us that there is something transcendental or, as Lewis writes in *The Four Loves*, something "eminently spiritual"[32] about the deepest friendships. Lewis writes that these rare friendships take on an "almost angelic relation and plunges into the depth of what is most natural and instinctive."[33] We see examples of these types of friendship in the Scriptures. In St. Paul's letter to Philemon, we learn about the relationship between Paul and Onesimus. Onesimus was Philemon's bondservant, and at some point Onesimus fled to Rome. While there, he met, befriended, and became useful to Paul. Now in his letter, Paul was sending the runaway bondservant Onesimus back to Philemon, telling Philemon that he would be personally responsible for anything Onesimus owed

29. Cigna 2018 Loneliness Index, https://www.cigna.com/assets/docs/ newsroom/loneliness-survey-2018-updated-fact-sheet.pdf.

30. National Academies, *Social Isolation and Loneliness*, xi.

31. Lewis, *Collected Letters*, 2:174

32. Lewis, *Four Loves*, 77.

33. Lewis, *Four Loves*, 78.

him. The relationship between the formerly "useless" Onesimus and the apostle Paul had developed to a level of friendship such that, in returning Onesimus, Paul writes, "I am sending him back to you, sending my very heart."[34] The Greek word Paul uses for "heart" means someone as dear as one's own self.

The heart St. Paul writes about when referring to Onesimus is the very core of the deepest friendships. As Onesimus was the very heart of Paul, Arthur was the heart of C. S. Lewis. In 1917, only three years into their friendship, Lewis composed a poem to his friend Arthur. "To the Memory of Arthur Greeves" concludes with the lines,

> Roaming – without a name- without a chart –
> The unknown garden of another's heart.

C. S. Lewis and Arthur Greeves were able to roam freely within the confines of each other's heart. The 296 letters from C. S. Lewis to Arthur Greeves and the unknown number of letters from Arthur to Lewis served as the thoroughfare providing access to each other's heart. No maps were ever necessary as, after fifty years of unveiling, of revealing, of confessing, of encouraging, and of loving, the topography was familiar terrain, with the natural out-working being that C. S. Lewis and Arthur Greeves were joined, as Lewis wrote, "like raindrops on a window."[35]

34. Philemon 12.
35. Lewis, *Surprised by Joy*, 199.

Bibliography

Augustine. *Confessions*. Translated by Albert C. Outler. New York: Barnes & Noble, 2007.

Austen, Jane. *Mansfield Park*. London: Macmillan, 1902.

Como, James T., ed. *C.S. Lewis at the Breakfast Table, and Other Reminiscences*. New York: Macmillan, 1979.

Davidman, Joy. *Out of My Bone: The Letters of Joy Davidman*. Edited by Don W. King. Grand Rapids: Eerdmans, 2009.

Dorsett, Lyle W. *And God Came In*. New York: Macmillan, 1883.

Downing, David C., and Michael G. Maudlin. *C.S. Lewis: The Reading Life: The Joy of Seeing Worlds through Other's Eyes*. New York: HarperOne, 2019.

Duriez, Colin. *The C.S. Lewis Encyclopedia*. New York: Inspirational, 2000.

Gibb, Jocelyn, ed. *Light on C. S. Lewis*. New York: Harcourt Brace Jovanovich, 1965.

Gresham, Douglas H. *Lenten Lands*. San Francisco: HarperSanFrancisco, 1988.

Hooper, Walter. *C.S. Lewis: A Companion & Guide*. London: HarperCollins, 1996.

———. *C.S. Lewis: A Complete Guide to His Life and Works*. London: HarperCollins, 2005.

Lewis, C. S. *All My Road Before Me: The Diary of C.S. Lewis, 1922–1927*. San Diego: Harcourt Brace Jovanovich, 1991.

———. *Allegory of Love*. Cambridge: Cambridge University Press, 2013.

———. *The Best of C.S. Lewis*. New York: Iversen, 1969.

———. *The Collected Letters of C.S. Lewis*. Edited by Walter Hooper. 3 vols. San Francisco: HarperSanFrancisco, 2007.

———., ed. *Essays Presented to Charles Williams*. Grand Rapids: Eerdmans, 1966.

———. *An Experiment in Criticism*. Cambridge: Cambridge University Press, 2013.

———. *The Four Loves*. San Diego: Harcourt Brace Jovanovich, 1988.

———. *Letters to Malcolm: Chiefly on Prayer*. New York: Harcourt, Brace & World, 1964.

———. *The Lion, the Witch, and the Wardrobe*. New York: HarperTrophy, 2002.

————. *Mere Christianity.* New York: HarperOne, 2001.

————. *Of Other Worlds.* Edited by Walter Hooper. New York: Harcourt Brace & World, 1966.

————. *The Pilgrim's Regress.* Edited by David C. Downing. Grand Rapids: Eerdmans, 2014.

————. *The Screwtape Letters.* New York: Iverson Associates, 1969.

————. *Surprised by Joy.* New York: Harcourt Brace Jovanovich, 1955.

————. *They Stand Together: The Letters of C.S. Lewis to Arthur Greeves (1914–1963).* Edited by Walter Hooper. New York, Macmillan, 1979.

————. *The Weight of Glory.* New York: HarperOne, 2001.

Jacobs, Alan. *The Narnian: The Life and Imagination of C.S. Lewis.* San Francisco: HarperSanFrancisco, 2005.

McGrath, Alister E. *C.S. Lewis: A Life: Eccentric Genius, Reluctant Prophet.* Carol Stream, IL: Tyndale House, 2013.

National Academies of Sciences, Engineering, and Medicine. *Social Isolation and Loneliness in Older Adults: Opportunities for the Health Care System.* Washington, DC: National Academies Press, 2020..

Pearce, Joseph. *The Unmasking of Oscar Wilde.* San Francisco: Ignatius, 2000.

Poe, Harry Lee. *Becoming C.S. Lewis: A Biography of Young Jack Lewis (1898–1918).* Wheaton, IL: Crossway, 2019.

Sayer, George. *Jack: A Life of C.S. Lewis.* London: Hodder & Stoughton, 1997.

Tolkien, J. R. R. *The Letters of J.R.R. Tolkien.* Edited by Humphrey Carpenter and Christopher Tolkien. Boston: Houghton Mifflin, 2000.

Zaleski, Philip, and Carol Zaleski. *The Fellowship: The Literary Lives of the Inklings.* New York: Farrar, Straus, & Giroux, 2015.